¡Ven conmigo!®

Holt Spanish
Level 1

Practice and Activity
Book

HOLT, RINEHART AND WINSTON
Harcourt Brace & Company
Austin • New York • Orlando • Atlanta • San Francisco • Boston • Dallas • Toronto • London

Contributing Writers:

Jean Miller
Dana Todd

Contents

¡Ven conmigo a Puerto Rico!

CAPÍTULO 11 Para vivir bien

CAPÍTULO 12 Las vacaciones ideales

En mi cuaderno

¡ADELANTE!

1 How would you respond to each of the following questions or statements? First, write in the missing Spanish punctuation marks. Then, write your responses and practice them aloud.

___Cómo te llamas?

___Buenos días!

¿Cómo se dice "*I have a question*" en español___

1. _____

2. _____

3. _____

___Cómo se escribe *burro*___

¡Buenas tardes___

¿XrüxKi?

4. _____

5. _____

6. _____

_____

2 Unscramble each of the following words to reveal the name of a Spanish-speaking country. Refer to the maps on pages xxiv and xxv of your textbook if you need help.

1. RHNOUASD _____

2. ZLAEVUEEN _____

3. ELCHI _____

4. MÁNPAA _____

5. GANTIENAR _____

6. TUGMLAEAA _____

7. ARANGCIAU _____

8. YUGRUAU _____

9. MOBICLOA _____

10. LE AVSLDOAR _____

11. GRAUYAPA _____

12. DOCUREA _____

13. TOASC ICAR _____

14. LVOBIIA _____

15. RÚPE _____

3 When you travel in a Spanish-speaking country you'll have to know how to fill out forms with your name and address. Answer the following questions.

1. ¿Cómo se escribe tu nombre completo? _____

2. ¿Cómo se escribe el nombre de tu calle *(street)*? _____

3. ¿Cómo se escribe el nombre de tu ciudad *(city)*? _____

4. ¿Cómo se escribe el nombre de tu estado *(state)*? _____

4 Imagine that you're mixing paints. What two colors would you mix to get the following results? Be sure to include the definite article **el** *(the)* with each color.

1. _____ + _____ = el morado

2. _____ + _____ = el anaranjado

3. _____ + _____ = el verde

4. _____ + _____ = el rosado

5. _____ + _____ = el gris

5 Use the Spanish words you've been learning to fill out the following crossword puzzle.

Horizontales (*Across*)

4. country in Central America, just north of Costa Rica
6. country in South America, between Chile and Uruguay
10. veinticinco – ocho = _____
11. Spanish boy's name, Nacho for short
12. cherries are this color
13. ocho – siete = _____

Verticales (*Down*)

1. chocolate is this color
2. diecisiete – trece = _____
3. veintiséis – once = _____
4. doce – tres = _____
5. broccoli is this color
7. rojo + blanco = _____
8. veintidós + ocho = _____
9. _____ + azul = verde

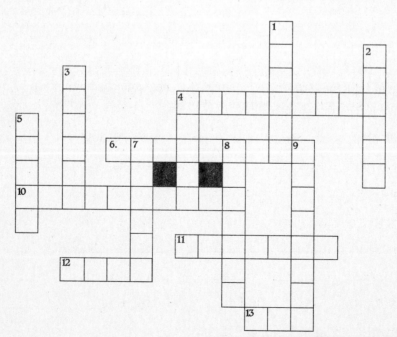

Nombre _____ Clase _____ Fecha _____

1 ¡Mucho gusto!

■ DE ANTEMANO

1 Look at the letter that Mercedes sent to Paco on page 19 of your textbook. Use the words and phrases in the box to write a short introduction for each of the two students shown below.

> ■ Soy de... Me llamo... Tengo ... años. Me gusta...

Juan Carlos/
San Sebastián/
16 años/
el voleibol

_____
_____
_____
_____

María Ángeles/
Santo Domingo/
14 años/
la pizza

_____
_____
_____
_____

2 Now look carefully at how Paco and his friends greet one another. Choose words and phrases from the box to complete the following dialogues. Use each word or phrase only once.

> ■ Excelente, gracias. ¿Y tú?   Adiós.   ¡Hola! ¿Qué tal?
> Buenos días.

1. PACO   Hasta luego, María.

    MARÍA   _____

2. JAVIER   _____

    CONSUELO   Hola, Javier. ¿Qúe tal?

3. MARTA   Hola, Gerardo. ¿Cómo estás?

    GERARDO   _____

4. PABLO   _____

    FERNANDO   Muy bien, Pablo, ¿y tú?

◼ PRIMER PASO

3 Match each of the following short conversations with the pictures. Write in the blank the letter of the picture that corresponds to the conversation.

a.   b.   c.

_____ **1.** — Bueno, tengo que irme. Hasta luego.

— ¡Chao!

_____ **2.** — Buenas tardes, señora Sánchez.

— Hola, Marisa.

_____ **3.** — Hola, señorita Martínez.

— Buenas noches.

4 Write the letter of an appropriate response in the blank next to each statement or question. Some responses may be used more than once.

If someone said . . .

_____ **1.** ¿Cómo te llamas?

_____ **2.** Éste es Felipe.

_____ **3.** Encantado.

_____ **4.** Hasta luego.

_____ **5.** Me llamo Conchita.

A logical response would be . . .

a. Adiós.

b. Igualmente.

c. Me llamo Conchita.

d. Encantado.

e. Mucho gusto.

f. ¡Hola!

g. Hasta luego.

5 A number of people have just been asked **¿Cómo estás?** First, punctuate the phrases and add any missing accents. Then match each of their responses with the letter of the drawing that best expresses how each person is doing.

a.   b.   c.

_____ 1. __Estoy excelente!

_____ 2. Estoy regular__

_____ 3. Bien__ gracias.

_____ 4. Estoy muy mal.

_____ 5. Estoy muy bien.

_____ 6. ¡Estupendo__

_____ 7. Mas o menos.

_____ 8. Regular, __y tu?

6 You have learned several phrases to say hello, to introduce yourself, to ask someone's name, to ask how someone feels, and to tell how you feel. Match these phrases to one of the two pictures of Teresa, according to whether she is talking about herself or talking to you.

a.   b.

_____ 1. Me llamo Teresa.   _____ 5. ¿Qué tal?

_____ 2. Encantada.   _____ 6. Estoy regular.

_____ 3. Hasta mañana.   _____ 7. ¿Cómo estás?

_____ 4. Estoy bien.   _____ 8. Yo soy Teresa.

7 Read the numbered phrases or questions below and decide which statement (**a** to **e**) applies to each one. Follow the **modelo**.

I should use this phrase . . .
  a. to find out information
  b. to greet someone
  c. to introduce myself
  d. when I have just met someone
  e. to say goodbye to someone

MODELO   __e__   **Adiós.**

_____ 1. Hola.

_____ 2. Yo soy...

_____ 3. Hasta luego.

_____ 4. Encantado/a.

_____ 5. Yo me llamo...

_____ 6. Buenas tardes.

_____ 7. Ésta es...

_____ 8. ¿Cómo te llamas?

_____ 9. Igualmente.

_____ 10. Mucho gusto.

8 It's the first day of school, so there are a lot of people meeting each other for the first time! For each of the following pictures, fill in the blanks to complete the conversations.

1. MARTÍN   Hola. _____

     NURIA   Me llamo Nuria.

     MARTÍN   Y yo soy Martín.

2. NURIA   _____

     _____

     MARTÍN   Igualmente.

3. LUCILA   _____

     _____

     MANUEL   Hola, Jesús. Mucho gusto.

4. JESÚS   _____

     _____

5. MANUEL   Bien, gracias, ¿y _____?

Nombre _____ Clase _____ Fecha _____

■ SEGUNDO PASO

9 Write out these math problems following the **modelo**.

MODELO $2 + 8 =$ **Dos y ocho son diez.**

1. $4 + 15 =$ _____

_____

2. $12 + 3 =$ _____

_____

3. $6 + 20 =$ _____

_____

4. $11 + 13 =$ _____

_____

5. $27 + 1 =$ _____

_____

6. $14 + 16 =$ _____

_____

10 Look at each of the illustrations below. Write a sentence asking or telling the age of each of the people shown.

1. Cristina   2. Rodolfo   3. Leonardo   4. Silvia   5. tú

1. ¿_____?

2. _____

3. ¿_____?

4. _____

5. _____

HRW material copyrighted under notice appearing earlier in this work.

11 School has just started, and two new students, Pilar and Verónica, are talking about some of the others they've met so far. Complete their conversation by filling in the missing forms of the verbs **tener** and **ser**.

PILAR ¿Cuántos años _____ Marcos?

VERÓNICA Dieciséis años.

PILAR ¿Y tú, Verónica? ¿Cuántos años _____?

VERÓNICA Yo _____ quince años.

PILAR ¿Sí? Yo también. Oye, Vero, ¿de dónde _____ tú?

VERÓNICA _____ de Monterrey, México.

PILAR ¡Yo también! ¿Y Matilde?

VERÓNICA Matilde _____ de Santa Fe de Bogotá, Colombia.

12 Choose the correct question word to complete the conversations.

cuántos
cómo   **dónde**

MARÍA Buenos días, Antonio. ¿ _____ estás?

ANTONIO Estoy bastante bien, gracias.

PEDRO ¿De _____ es Jean?

JULIA Es de los Estados Unidos.

ANA ¿ _____ se llama él?

CARLOS Se llama Juanito.

ESTÉBAN Oye, Irene, ¿ _____ años tiene Pablo?

IRENE Tiene catorce años.

13 Mike is a seventeen-year-old exchange student from Michigan living in Madrid. On his first day of classes Maribel strikes up a conversation. Complete their conversation.

1. MARIBEL Hola, soy Maribel. ¿Cómo te llamas tú?

    MIKE _____

2. MARIBEL Encantada, Mike.

    MIKE _____

3. MARIBEL Tú no eres de Madrid, ¿verdad? ¿_____?

    MIKE Soy de Estados Unidos.

4. MARIBEL ¿Y cuántos años tienes?

    MIKE _____

5. MARIBEL Bueno, Mike, tengo que irme. ¡Chao!

    MIKE _____

■ TERCER PASO

14 Whatever Beto likes, Memo doesn't like, and whatever Memo likes, Beto doesn't. Fill in the missing parts of each boy's statements according to the pictures.

Beto

1. BETO ¿_____ gusta?

   MEMO A mí _____ el tenis.

2. BETO _____ gusta el fútbol

   norteamericano.

   MEMO A mí _____ el fútbol

   norteamericano.

3. _____ ¿_____ la natación?

   MEMO A mí _____ mucho la

   natación.

   BETO Pues a mí no me gusta _____ .

5. MEMO _____ el fútbol.

   BETO _____ el béisbol.

   MEMO _____ el béisbol.

6. BETO _____ el baloncesto.

   MEMO ¡A mí también!

Memo

15 You can put either **el** or **la** before every noun you've learned so far. Read the following short interview between *Estrella* magazine and Juanito Serrano, a young pop singer. Complete the interview by filling in the blanks with either **el** or **la**.

E   Juanito, ¿qué te gusta?

JS ¿Qué me gusta? Bueno, me gusta un poco de todo *(a little bit of everything)*.

E   ¿Te gusta _____ pizza?

JS Sí, me gusta, pero me gusta más _____ comida china. ¡Y _____ chocolate!

E   ¿Y deportes *(sports)*?

JS Bueno, me gusta _____ baloncesto, y también _____ natación. No me gusta _____

   voleibol.

E   ¿Qué más? *(What else?)*

JS Bueno, me gusta mucho _____ música rock y clásica. Y _____ clase de inglés me gusta

   mucho también, pero no me gusta _____ tarea.

CAPÍTULO 1 Tercer paso

16 a. For each category given below, choose an item that you like and write a sentence saying that you like it. Then choose another item and write a sentence saying that you don't like it. Be sure to write **el** or **la** in front of the name of each item.

la natación   la tarea   la comida italiana

la música rock   el fútbol   la ensalada

el béisbol   el chocolate   la música clásica

el español   la clase de inglés   el jazz

La música: _____

La comida: _____

Los deportes: _____

Las clases: _____

b. Now choose two items from one category above and write a question asking a friend which of the two he or she likes better. Then write your friend's answer.

_____

_____

17 Heather is practicing her Spanish with Antonio, the new exchange student from Spain. Based on Antonio's answers, supply the questions Heather asked him.

HEATHER _____

ANTONIO Me llamo Antonio Carreras Llosa.

HEATHER _____

ANTONIO Estoy bien, gracias.

HEATHER _____

ANTONIO Tengo diecisiete años.

HEATHER _____

ANTONIO Soy de Barcelona, España.

18 You've just gotten a pen pal from Spain, Maricarmen Martínez García. Write her a short letter. Tell her about yourself: your name, how you are, how old you are, where you're from, and what you like and don't like. Close your letter by saying goodbye. Be sure to ask your pen pal questions about herself too. (Begin your letter **Querida Maricarmen**, *Dear Maricarmen,*)

_____

_____

_____

_____

_____

¡Ven conmigo! Level 1, Chapter 1

VAMOS A LEER

19 Imagine that your pen pal Maricarmen has sent you a reply to your first letter. Read her letter, then answer the following questions.

> Hola,
>
> Muchas gracias por tu carta tan agradable. Ya sabes que me llamo Maricarmen. Pues, ¿sabes mis apellidos? Soy Maricarmen Martínez García. Tengo quince años y soy estudiante. Soy de Madrid. Madrid es la capital de España y es una ciudad maravillosa. Me gusta Madrid porque siempre hay muchas cosas interesantes que hacer. También me gusta el fútbol. No me gusta el fútbol norteamericano. ¡Es difícil de entender! Pero sí me gusta la música norteamericana. La música pop es estupenda, ¿sabes? Tengo varios discos compactos de Janet Jackson, Chris Isaak y REM. También me gustan las películas de Hollywood. La actriz norteamericana que más me gusta es Wynona Rider. También me gusta el actor Arnold Schwarzenegger. Bueno, espero recibir una carta tuya muy pronto. ¡Hasta luego!
>
> Tu amiga
> Maricarmen

1. List the names of any places you can find.

   _____

2. List any names of sports you can find.

   _____

3. List at least three things that Maricarmen likes.

   _____

   _____

   _____

4. List one thing Maricarmen doesn't like.

   _____

5. Judging from its context, what do you think the word **películas** means?

   _____

6. What do you have in common with Maricarmen?

   _____

■ CULTURA

20 Typically, people in Spanish-speaking countries have a **nombre** (*first name*) and two **apellidos** (*last names*). Where do those last names come from? Here is Maricarmen's family tree, complete with all the **nombres** and **apellidos** of her parents and grandparents. Look at the names in the family tree, then answer the questions.

Juan Carlos   María Elena   Lorenzo   Isabel
Martínez Gómez   Blanco de Martínez   García Vázquez   Torres de García

Vicente   Mariano   Soledad
Martínez Blanco   Martínez Blanco   García Torres (de Martínez)

Maricarmen
Martínez García

1. What is Maricarmen's father's full name? _____

2. What is Maricarmen's uncle's full name? _____

3. What is Maricarmen's mother's full name? _____

4. Which names did Maricarmen take from each of her parents? _____

_____

5. If you were to go to Madrid, and wanted to call up Maricarmen, what name would you

look under in the Madrid phone book? _____

21 a. Spanish-speaking people greet each other differently than many people in the United States. Decide whether the following statements are **cierto** (*true*) or **falso** (*falso*).

1. _____ Friends in Spain often greet each other with a kiss on both cheeks.

2. _____ Like Spaniards, Latin Americans kiss each other on both cheeks when saying hello.

3. _____ Young people in Spanish-speaking countries often shake hands when meeting or when saying goodbye.

4. _____ Spanish-speaking men only shake hands when greeting one another.

5. _____ In Spanish-speaking cultures, family members usually greet each other with a handshake.

b. How do you, your family, and your friends normally greet each other? How is this different from the way Spanish-speakers customarily greet each other? Is one more "formal" than the other? more "friendly"? How far apart do you stand or sit from each other?

_____

_____

_____

_____

_____

Nombre _____ Clase _____ Fecha _____

¡Organízate!

■ DE ANTEMANO

1 You're a clerk at the school store, and one of your customers asks you to help him check his bill. Next to each price on the ticket, write the item it represents.

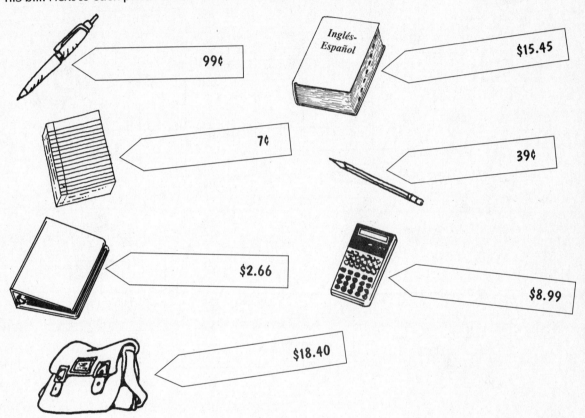

2 It's the first day of classes and the bookstore is crowded. You overhear the following conversations. Can you match each question and answer?

_____ 1. ¿Qué necesitas?

_____ 2. ¿Tienes una calculadora?

_____ 3. ¿Necesitas cuadernos?

_____ 4. ¿Tienes papel?

_____ 5. ¿Tienes zapatillas de tenis?

_____ 6. ¿Necesitas más bolígrafos?

_____ 7. ¿Ya tienes una mochila?

a. Sí, ya tengo una calculadora.
b. No, no tengo mochila.
c. No, ya tengo muchos bolígrafos.
d. No, no necesito cuadernos. Ya tengo tres.
e. ¡Ay, necesito muchas cosas!
f. No, no tengo papel. Necesito papel y también unos lápices.
g. Sí, tengo unas zapatillas de tenis.

PRIMER PASO

3 The Librería San Martín will give away a year's supply of pens to the first customer to complete this crossword puzzle. Write in the Spanish words for the items pictured below. Include the correct definite article with each item.

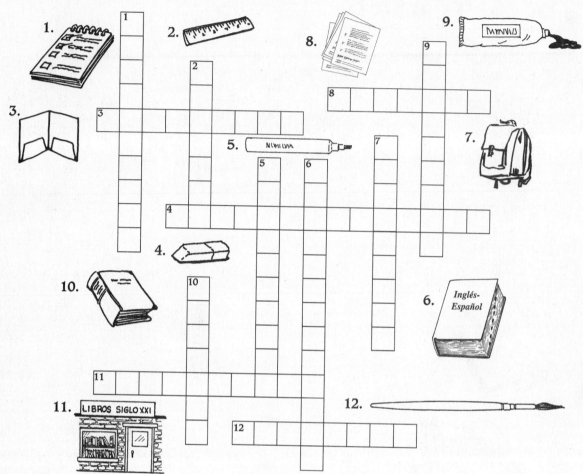

4 Complete the conversation between Guillermo and the bookstore clerk with the correct indefinite articles (**un** or **una**) and the word for each item pictured.

DEPENDIENTE Hola, buenos días. ¿Qué necesita?

   GUILLERMO Hola. Por favor, necesito _____.

DEPENDIENTE Muy bien. ¿Algo más?

   GUILLERMO Sí. Necesito _____, _____ y

                   _____.

DEPENDIENTE ¡Necesita muchas cosas!

   GUILLERMO Sí. También necesito _____, _____ y

 _____. ¡Y ahora necesito dinero!

¡Ven conmigo! Level 1, Chapter 2

5 Choose four of the students in the illustration. For each one, write a question asking what the student wants or needs. Then answer the question. In your answers, use **él** and **ella** instead of the customer's names.

Horacio   Lourdes   Amalia   Martín   Teresa   Ricardo   Alejandro

1. (necesitar) _____

_____

2. (necesitar) _____

_____

3. (querer) _____

_____

4. (necesitar) _____

_____

6 Imagine that you're also in the bookstore above and you need four different items. Complete the conversation you might have with the clerk.

1. Buenas tardes. ¿ _____?

2. Necesito _____

3. ¿Ya tienes _____?

4. _____

5. ¿Quieres _____?

7 You work in the lost-and-found office at school and someone has just turned in a lost bookbag. Fill out a report by describing the contents.

MODELO   **En la mochila hay una regla. También hay...**

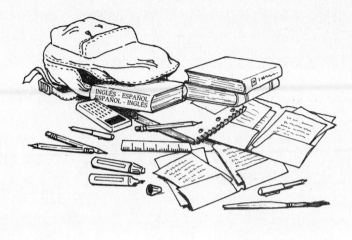

_____

_____

_____

_____

_____

_____

8 You found a new job at a bookstore. The store is overstocked with school supplies and you've got to try to sell them all. Use all the words from the box to make sentences asking your customers if they need, already have, or want what you're trying to sell. Don't forget to include the proper indefinite article when necessary.

diccionario   calculadora   papel   regla   cuadernos
   lápices   carpetas   gomas de borrar   libros   mochila   bolígrafos

_____

_____

_____

_____

_____

_____

_____

_____

_____

_____

CAPÍTULO 2 Primer paso

¡Ven conmigo! Level 1, Chapter 2

■ SEGUNDO PASO

9 A friend of yours has decided to learn Spanish too. To learn vocabulary, your friend is making labels for everything in the bedroom. Help your friend by writing the correct Spanish word on each label. Remember to include the correct definite article.

bed _____	*chair* _____
window _____	*clothes* _____
door _____	*closet* _____
poster _____	*television* _____
clock _____	*desk* _____

10 Fede and Juanjo are best friends, but as you can see from their rooms, they're very different! List what each has in his room according to the drawing.

En el cuarto de Fede, hay...

En el cuarto de Juanjo, hay...

_____

_____

_____

_____

_____

11 Your pen pal Lucila has just moved to a new city and has written a letter to you about her school, her classes, and her room in her new apartment. Complete her letter with the correct form of **mucho** or **cuánto.**

Querido amigo,

¡Hola! ¿Cómo estás? Yo estoy bien. Tengo **1.** _____ amigos aquí.

2. ¿ _____ amigos tienes tú?

Mi colegio nuevo es muy grande, pero me gusta. Hay **3.** _____ estudiantes. **4.** ¿ _____ estudiantes hay en tu colegio? Tengo ocho clases.

5. ¿ _____ clases tienes tú? Mi clase favorita es la clase de inglés. No hay **6.** _____ personas en la clase. **7.** ¿ _____ personas hay en tu clase de inglés? No me gusta la clase de álgebra. Es difícil. Hay

8. _____ tarea y **9.** _____ exámenes. ¿Te gusta la clase de álgebra?

Vivo en un apartamento nuevo. Me gusta mucho mi cuarto. En mi cuarto, hay **10.** _____ ventanas. Y también tengo **11.** _____ carteles de mis actores favoritos. **12.** ¿ _____ hay en tu cuarto?

Bueno, necesito ir a la librería ahora. Necesito comprar **13.** _____ libros para mis clases. ¡Pero no tengo **14.** _____ dinero!

¡Hasta luego!

Lucila

12 Write a letter back to Lucila, remembering to answer her questions. Include any other information you like about your school, your classes, or your room. Also, ask her what there is in her room and if she has a TV set.

_____

_____

_____

_____

_____

_____

_____

_____

_____

_____

_____

13 Flavia Martínez Campos is a new exchange student from Mexico at your school this year. There are a lot of things that she wants to know about school. Help her out by answering the following questions with full sentences.

MODELO   FLAVIA   ¿Cuántos profesores hay en el colegio?
                   TÚ   **Hay treinta y un profesores en el colegio.**

1. ¿Cuántos estudiantes hay en tu clase de español?

    _____

    _____

2. ¿Qué necesito para mi clase de inglés?

    _____

    _____

3. ¿Cómo se llama el director del colegio *(principal)*?

    _____

    _____

4. ¿Te gusta la comida de la cafetería? ¿Qué no te gusta?

    _____

    _____

5. ¿Hay comida mexicana en la cafetería? ¿Hay ensalada?

    _____

    _____

6. ¿Cuánta tarea hay en la clase de inglés?

    _____

    _____

7. ¿Necesito una calculadora?

    _____

    _____

8. ¿Tienes una mochila? Y yo, ¿necesito una mochila?

    _____

    _____

9. ¿Cuántos cuadernos necesito para las clases?

    _____

    _____

10. ¿Hay muchas revistas en español en la librería?

    _____

    _____

Nombre _____ Clase _____ Fecha _____

■ TERCER PASO

14 After school, you overhear a lot of different conversations going home on the bus. Can you match the questions with the answers?

_____ 1. ¿Qué quieres hacer?

_____ 2. ¿Necesitas ir a la librería?

_____ 3. ¿Qué quiere hacer Paco?

_____ 4. ¿Necesitas comprar muchas cosas en la librería?

a. Paco quiere ir al centro comercial.

b. Quiero ir a la pizzería. ¡La pizza es deliciosa!

c. No, ya tengo los libros. Ahora necesito organizar mi cuarto.

d. Sí... necesito comprar todo. Pero no tengo mucho dinero.

15 Look over the expressions in the **Así se dice** box on page 56 of your textbook. What phrase would you use to . . .?

1. ask a friend what he or she wants to do

_____

2. ask a customer in the bookstore what he or she needs to buy

_____

3. tell a friend you need to organize your room

_____

4. tell a friend you don't want to do your homework

_____

5. tell your parent or guardian what school supplies you need

_____

6. ask someone what Esteban wants to do

_____

7. say that you want to go to the pizzeria

_____

16 Carmen has just passed you a note in the hall about after-school plans, but part of the message is in code! Can you unscramble it and figure out what she's saying? Write the decoded version in the blanks beneath Carmen's note.

¡Lah o! Necesito zgroiaran im tucaro, rpeo ieqrou ri la centro lmeocriac. Nocsetie comprar cshuma socsa. ¿Uéq quieres chear út?

_____

_____

HRW material copyrighted under notice appearing earlier in this work.

17 It's the last period of the day, and everyone in Mr. Santos' class is thinking about after-school plans . . . including Mr. Santos! Answer the questions below about people's plans based on the drawing.

El profesor
Santos   Rosaura   Matilde   Óscar   Eduardo   Julia   Sofía   Mateo

1. ¿Qué necesita hacer el profesor Santos?

   _____

2. ¿Qué necesita encontrar Rosaura?

   _____

3. ¿Qué quiere comprar Óscar?

   _____

4. ¿Qué necesita hacer Julia?

   _____

5. ¿Qué quiere hacer Mateo?

   _____

6. ¿Qué necesita comprar Matilde?

   _____

7. ¿Qué necesita hacer Eduardo?

   _____

8. ¿Qué quiere hacer Sofía?

   _____

CAPÍTULO 2 Tercer paso

18 It's been a while since Lupe has cleaned her room. Now she's got a lot of work ahead of her. Make a list of at least five things she needs to do, according to the drawing.

_____

_____

_____

_____

_____

19 You've just finished helping out with the school inventory, and now it's time to report to your supervisor. Answer her questions about what's in the supply room according to the inventory sheet.

libros	81	cuadernos	92
televisores	12	diccionarios	41
carteles	59	sillas	61
lámparas	38	escritorios	77

MODELO   ¿Cuántos libros hay?
             Hay ochenta y un libros.

1. ¿Cuántos televisores hay? _____

   _____

2. ¿Cuántas lámparas hay? _____

   _____

3. ¿Cuántos cuadernos hay? _____

   _____

4. ¿Cuántos diccionarios hay? _____

   _____

5. ¿Cuántas sillas hay? _____

   _____

6. ¿Cuántos escritorios hay? _____

   _____

7. ¿Cuántos carteles hay? _____

   _____

■ VAMOS A LEER

20 You're waiting in line to buy your school supplies at the **Librería San Martín**, and it's taking forever. While you wait, look over the magazines on display, and see if you can answer the questions below.

a.

b.

c.

d.

Can you figure out what topics are covered in each magazine just by looking at the covers? Match each magazine to the topics below.

_____ 1. Science and technology

_____ 2. Homemaking ideas

_____ 3. Gossip about celebrities

_____ 4. Current events

Front cover from *Epoca*, no. 118, September 6, 1993. Reprinted by permission of **Epoca de México, S.A. de C.V.**; Front cover from *Mi familia y yo*, no. 41, July-August 1993. Reprinted by permission of **Family Circle S.A.**; Front cover from *On Off*, no. 15. Reprinted by permission of **On Off**; Front cover from *Diez Minutos*, año XLIII, 1993. Reprinted by permission of **Hachette Filipacchi**.

◼ CULTURA

21 Juan Antonio, a student from Spain, will be coming to live with the McRae family for a whole year. The McRaes have two teenagers, Mike and Jennifer, and live in a house in a small town. While staying with them, Juan Antonio will have his own large room. He'll share a TV and a phone with Mike and Jennifer. Using what you've learned about many Spanish homes, what aspects of his life with the McRaes do you think will seem strange to Juan Antonio?

_____

_____

_____

_____

_____

_____

22 Juan Antonio will be attending the local high school while he's living with the McRaes. After a week of school, he's writing a letter to his best friend back home. Keeping in mind what you learned about how life is in the Spanish-speaking world, what observations do you think Juan Antonio would make to his friend about high school in the United States?

_____

_____

_____

_____

_____

_____

CAPÍTULO **3**

Nuevas clases, nuevos amigos

DE ANTEMANO

1 As you know, it's Claudia's first day at her new school, and everybody—including Claudia—
has lots of questions! See if you can match everybody's questions and answers in the
columns below.

_____ 1. ¿Cómo te llamas?

_____ 2. ¿Cómo es el profesor Romanca?

_____ 3. ¿Qué clase tienes a las ocho y cincuenta?

_____ 4. ¿Cuándo es el descanso?

_____ 5. ¿De dónde eres?

_____ 6. ¿Cómo es la capital?

a. Yo tengo francés y Fernando tiene
   geografía.
b. Soy del Distrito Federal.
c. Me llamo María Inés. Encantada.
d. Es aburrido. ¡No me gusta!
e. Es muy divertida. Hay muchas
   cosas interesantes allá. Me gusta
   mucho.
f. Es a las nueve y cuarenta.

2 Match the following pictures with the comments.

1. _____

2. _____

3. _____

a. Muy bien, a las ocho tengo francés, y a las nueve tengo la clase de ciencias sociales...
b. Mira, ya son las diez y media. Está atrasada la profesora.
c. ¡No me gustan las ciencias sociales!

CAPÍTULO 3 De antemano

■ PRIMER PASO

3 Use the pictures to fill in the classes that Ángela is taking this semester. Then rearrange the circled letters to find out what Ángela's favorite class is.

1. ⬚ⓞⅡⅡⅡⅡⅡⅡ

2. ⓞⅡⅡ

3. ⅡⅡⅡⅡⅡⓞⅡ
   ⅡⅡⓞⅡ

4. 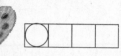 ⅡⅡⅡⅡⅡⓞⅡⅡ

5. ⓞⅡⅡⅡⅡⅡⅡⅡⓞ

6. ⅡⅡⅡⅡⅡⅡⅡⓞ

La clase favorita de Ángela es la clase de ___ __ __ __ __ __ __ __ __ .

4 Look at Juan's class schedule, then complete his conversation with Mari using the words in the box.

> mañana   luego   hoy   por fin   primero

viernes	sábado
química	
matemáticas	
alemán	
educación física	
almuerzo	
español	
computación	

MARI   Oye, Juan, ¿qué clases tienes _____?

JUAN   Bueno, _____ tengo la clase de

química. Después tengo_____,

_____ y _____.

_____ tengo el almuerzo, español,

y _____ la clase de computación.

MARI   ¿Y _____? ¿Qué clases tienes?

JUAN   Hombre, ¡el sábado es un día libre!

¡Ven conmigo! Level 1, Chapter 3

5 Claudia is writing a short letter to her friend Sonia, back in Mexico City, about her life in Cuernavaca. Complete her letter with the correct definite article: **el**, **la**, **los**, or **las**.

> Cuernavaca
> 8 de octubre del 1995
> Querida Sonia,
>
> ¿Cómo estás? Yo estoy muy bien aquí en Cuernavaca. Me gusta 1. _____ nuevo colegio.
> 2. _____ estudiantes son simpáticos e inteligentes. 3. _____ director se llama Sr.
> Altamirano. Este año, tengo nueve materias. 4. _____ clases de ciencias sociales y literatura
> son mis favoritas. Son muy interesantes. También me gusta 5. _____ clase de francés, pero
> necesito estudiar mucho. 6. _____ exámenes son difíciles. ¡Y 7. _____ tarea es horri-
> ble! Bueno, ahora necesito ir a 8. _____ librería. Quiero comprar 9. _____ libros para
> 10. _____ clases de geografía y biología. Después, voy a 11. _____ pizzería con mis
> amigos Fernando y María Inés.
> ¡Escríbeme pronto!
>
> > Un abrazo,
> > Claudia

6 Teresa and Patricia were passing a note in study hall about their afternoon classes and plans for after school. Can you put the pieces of their torn-up note back in order? Write the number of the sentence in the left-hand column next to the sentence in the right-hand column that goes with it.

1. Hola, Tere. ¿Qué clases tienes?	____ Sí, me gusta, pero nececesito estudiar mucho. Hay mucha tarea.
2. ¿Te gusta la clase?	____ Sí, gracias. Necesito estudiar también.
3. Y después, ¿qué clases tienes?	____ Bueno, primero tengo la clase de historia con el profesor Román.
4. Y después, ¿quieres ir al partido de basquetbol?	____ Sí, quiero, pero necesito estudiar.
5. ¿Quieres estudiar en mi casa?	____ Después tengo computación, ciencias y luego español.

CAPÍTULO 3 Primer paso

7 For each clock, write a question asking what time it is or if it's a certain time. Then answer the question.

1. _____ 2. _____ 3. _____

_____ _____ _____

4. _____ 5. _____ 6. _____

_____ _____ _____

8 Look at the series of pictures showing a typical day in the life of Esteban. What time of the day do you think it is when Esteban does all these things? First number the drawings 1-4, according to the order in which they happen. Then write a sentence in Spanish saying what time you think it is in each drawing,

_____ _____ _____ _____

1. _____

2. _____

3. _____

4. _____

CAPÍTULO 3 Primer paso

◼ SEGUNDO PASO

9 Beto and Lola are at the Pizzería Napolitana discussing the first day of classes. Complete their conversation with the words and expressions from the box. Some words or expressions may be used more than once.

| prisa | es a las | ¿a qué hora es? | atrasada | a las | son las | ¿qué hora es? |

BETO   ¿Qué clases tienes este semestre?

LOLA   Bueno, primero tengo álgebra _____ 8:45 de la mañana. Es una clase

interesante. Después, _____ 9:45 tengo geografía. Me gusta esa clase. Es divertida.

BETO   Tengo geografía también, pero mi clase _____ 2:30 de la tarde. Mi

clase favorita _____ 10:00 de la mañana. Es la clase de literatura. Hay mucha tarea en esa clase, pero me gusta.

LOLA   Necesitas comprar muchos libros para la clase, ¿verdad?

BETO   Sí. Necesito ir a la librería esta tarde _____ seis.

LOLA   Perdón, Beto... ¿_____ ahora?

BETO   _____ cuatro y veinticinco.

LOLA   ¡Es tarde! Estoy _____. Necesito ir a casa ahora mismo. Quiero ver (*to see*) mi programa de televisión favorito.

BETO   ¿Y _____ el programa?

LOLA   ¡_____ cuatro y media!

BETO   Entonces, ¡date _____!

10 Bárbara's made a list of things she's going to do today and when she's going to do them. First decide whether each item in her list is something she wants to do or something she needs to do. Then write a sentence stating what she needs or wants to do and at what time. Write out the times, and indicate morning, afternoon, or evening, as in the model.

MODELO   comprar lápices en la librería (3:00 P.M.)
           Bárbara necesita comprar lápices en la librería a las tres de la tarde.

1. ir al colegio (8:45 A.M.)

     _____

     _____

2. ir a la clase de español (9:50 A.M.)

     _____

     _____

3. ir a la pizzería (12:20 P.M.)

     _____

     _____

4. organizar el armario (3:30 P.M.)

_____

_____

5. comprar nuevas zapatillas de tenis (4:15 P.M.)

_____

_____

6. hacer la tarea para mañana (6:00 P.M.)

_____

_____

7. cenar (*to have dinner*) (8:15 P.M.)

_____

_____

8. ir con los amigos a una fiesta (*party*) (9:40 P.M.)

_____

_____

11 Once again, Carmen's late for an appointment, this time with Professor Sánchez. Complete the following conversation between her and Felipe with the appropriate word from the box. You may use some words more than once.

qué hora	ahora	atrasada	prisa	atrasado	date	en punto	a qué hora

FELIPE   Carmen, ¿por qué tienes 1. _____?

CARMEN   Es que estoy 2. _____.

FELIPE   Pero, ¿por qué? Es temprano.

CARMEN   Sí, pero necesito hablar (*to talk*) con el profesor Sánchez esta mañana.

FELIPE   ¿De veras? 3. ¿_____ necesitas hablar con él?

CARMEN   A las ocho 4. _____. ¿Sabes 5. _____ es, Felipe?

FELIPE   A ver. 6. _____ son las ocho y cinco.

CARMEN   ¡Ay, no! No puede ser. (*It can't be.*) Estoy muy 7. _____.

FELIPE   Pues, no te preocupes (*don't worry*). El profesor Sánchez siempre está

8. _____ también.

CARMEN   Sí, pero ya está en su oficina (*He's already in his office*).

FELIPE   9. ¡_____ prisa, Carmen! Hasta luego.

CARMEN   Adiós.

Nombre _____ Clase _____ Fecha _____

12 Rafael and Guillermo have run into each other in the hallway between classes. Write a short conversation between the two. Use the cues below as a guide.

Rafael

Greets Guillermo. Asks him how he is.

_____
_____

Says he's so-so. Asks if Guillermo wants to go to the movies today.

_____
_____

Says at 4:30 P.M.

_____
_____

Says very well. Asks what time it is.

_____
_____

Says that he's late, too. Tells Guillermo to hurry up.

_____
_____

Guillermo

Says fine, thanks, and asks about Rafael.

_____
_____

Says yes, and asks at what time.

_____
_____

Says yes, he wants to go, but first he needs to do his homework.

_____
_____

Says that it's 2:30. Says that he has class now. Says that he's late.

_____
_____

Says see you later.

_____
_____

13 Claudia is having a difficult first week at her new school! She and Profesor Garza just collided in the hallway, and now their stuff is all mixed up. Help sort things out by saying which things belong to which person, following the model below.

MODELO   La regla / Claudia
        La regla es de Claudia.

1. los exámenes / el profesor Garza _____

2. las carpetas / Claudia _____

3. el dinero / el profesor Garza _____

4. el sándwich / Claudia _____

5. la fruta / el profesor Garza _____

6. los libros / Claudia _____

7. los bolígrafos / el profesor Garza _____

HRW material copyrighted under notice appearing earlier in this work.

CAPÍTULO 3 Segundo paso

■ TERCER PASO

14 Write a question for each illustration below using the tag question forms you learned on page 88 of your textbook. The first one is done for you as a model.

mis amigos

Mis amigos son simpáticos,
¿verdad?

las clases

_____

_____

_____

los exámenes

_____

_____

_____

el Presidente de EEUU

_____

_____

_____

el monstruo

_____

_____

_____

los profesores

_____

_____

_____

15 Claudia and Fernando are having a snack after class in a café. Complete their conversation with the correct forms of the verb **ser** and any other words you need.

FERNANDO   Bueno, Claudia... ¿_____ tus clases?

CLAUDIA   ¡Uf! ¡Ya tengo mucha tarea! Las clases _____ difíciles en este colegio.

FERNANDO   Sí, aquí los profesores _____ muy estrictos.

CLAUDIA   Mi profesor de computación se llama Profesor Guzmán.

FERNANDO   ¡Ay! ¡Qué mala suerte! (*what rotten luck!*) Él _____ muy estricto.

CLAUDIA   ¿Y _____ la profesora de historia?

FERNANDO   ¿La profesora Ureña? Bueno, _____ inteligente y divertida. Pero la clase no

_____ fácil. Necesitas estudiar mucho.

CLAUDIA   Y hay un profesor de biología... no sé cómo se llama. _____ alto, **guapo** y

moreno.

FERNANDO   Ah, el profesor Chamorro. Es muy inteligente y la clase de biología _____

super-interesante.

CLAUDIA   Bueno, tengo que irme. Necesito hacer la tarea para mañana.

FERNANDO   Claudia, no te preocupes (*Don't worry!*). Tú _____ muy inteligente.

16 Complete the sentences below by circling the two adjectives that correctly match the subject of each sentence.

1. La profesora Alonso es...
   a. inteligentes   **b.** baja   **c.** moreno   **d.** simpática

2. Las novelas de Mark Twain son...
   a. difícil   **b.** cómicas   **c.** interesantes   **d.** aburrida

3. Mi amigo Roberto es...
   a. guapo   **b.** cómica   **c.** alta   **d.** rubio

4. Las fiestas del Club de español son...
   a. grandes   **b.** aburrido   **c.** divertidas   **d.** buena

5. Los estudiantes de mi colegio son...
   a. bueno   **b.** guapos   **c.** inteligentes   **d.** antipática

6. La clase de química es...
   a. interesantes   **b.** fáciles   **c.** divertida   **d.** difícil

7. La tarea para mañana es...
   a. horrible   **b.** divertidas   **c.** fáciles   **d.** aburrida

8. Mi perro (*dog*) Max es...
   a. malos   **b.** cómico   **c.** fea   **d.** bonito

CAPÍTULO 3 Tercer paso

17 Fill in the blanks of the sentences below with the correct form of the adjectives in parentheses.

1. Mi clase favorita es la geografía porque es _____ (interesante).

2. La profesora de español es muy _____ (estricto).

3. No me gustan las clases _____ (aburrido).

4. Todos *(All)* mis amigos son _____ (simpático).

5. Para mí, los videojuegos son muy _____ (divertido).

6. No me gustan los exámenes de matemáticas porque son _____ (difícil).

7. María estudia *(studies)* mucho; es muy _____ (inteligente).

8. Mi amiga Berta es _____ (bonito).

18 Your little brother won't stop asking questions! Get him off your back by answering the questions below. Base your answers on your opinions of the things mentioned.

MODELO —¿Por qué te gusta la clase de español?
—Me gusta porque es divertida.

1. ¿Por qué no te gustan los exámenes?

   _____

2. ¿Por qué te gustan los deportes?

   _____

3. ¿Por qué te gustan los conciertos?

   _____

4. ¿Por qué te gusta el profesor Román?

   _____

19 Complete the sentences below using adjectives from the reading on page 35 with the correct form of **ser**. Remember to make the adjective match its subject!

Yo... _____

Mis amigos y yo... _____

Mi familia... _____

El profesor/La profesora de español... _____

Los estudiantes de la clase de español... _____

Tú _____

Nosotros _____

¡Ven conmigo! Level 1, Chapter 3

◼ VAMOS A LEER

20 Do you have a favorite color? Do you think that someone's favorite color is an indication of his or her personality? Read the article below, then answer the questions. (HINT: If you've forgotten the colors, see page 9 of your textbook.)

Analiza el "color" de tu personalidad

Rojo	Si te gusta el rojo, entonces eres impulsivo(a), impaciente y extrovertido(a).
Azul	¿Prefieres el azul? Pues, probablemente eres conservador(a), serio(a) e intelectual.
Verde	Si te gusta el verde, eres una persona paciente, generosa y tolerante.
Amarillo	El amarillo es el color de las personas optimistas e idealistas. Si prefieres el amarillo, probablemente eres muy activo(a) también.
Anaranjado	¿Prefieres este color? Entonces eres sociable, realista y honesto(a).
Morado	Éste es el color de las personas artísticas, temperamentales y románticas.

One of the reading strategies you've practiced is working with cognates. You probably noticed some cognates as you were reading through this article. Find the Spanish cognates of these English adjectives:

honest
_____

impulsive
_____

serious
_____

generous
_____

intellectual
_____

active
_____

temperamental
_____

sociable
_____

extroverted
_____

¡Ven conmigo! Level 1, Chapter 3

Practice and Activity Book **35**

HRW material copyrighted under notice appearing earlier in this work.

CAPÍTULO 3 Vamos a leer

■ CULTURA

21 People from the U.S. have a reputation in other countries for always being on time. Is that reputation true, or is it a stereotype? Is it ever all right to be late in this country? Make a list of three occasions when it's acceptable to arrive late, and three when it's necessary to be on time. Can you make any generalizations about your lists, and about attitudes towards time in the U.S.? How do your attitudes towards time differ from those in Spanish-speaking cultures?

_____

_____

_____

_____

_____

_____

_____

22 Below are some expressions you can use when someone tells you what grade he or she got:

> **¡Qué bien!** *That's great!*
> **Lo siento.** *I'm sorry.*

React to each student's comment about his or her grade using one of the expressions above. Base your reaction on what you learned about grading in Spanish-speaking countries.

MODELO   Isabel (México, D.F.)   Saqué (*I got*) un 10 en la clase de química.
            Tú   ¡Qué bien!

1. Gabriela (Oaxaca, México): Saqué un 8 en la clase de geometría.

   Tú: _____

2. Mariana (Lima, Perú): Saqué un 17 en la clase de inglés.

   Tú: _____

3. Felipe (Ciudad Juárez, México): Saqué un 5 en la clase de álgebra.

   Tú: _____

4. Daniela (Arequipa, Perú): Saqué un 12 en la clase de literatura.

   Tú: _____

5. Xóchitl (Jalisco, México): Saqué un 9 en la clase de computación.

   Tú: _____

6. José Alberto (Iquitos, Perú): Saqué un 19 en la clase de biología.

   Tú: _____

4 ¿Qué haces esta tarde?

■ DE ANTEMANO

1 As you saw in the **fotonovela**, everybody has a lot of questions. Match the different questions and answers below.

_____ 1. Luis, ¿vas a Taxco con Claudia y Rosa?

a. Por lo general estudia en la biblioteca.

_____ 2. ¿Dónde está el correo?

b. Sí, le gusta mucho. Los sábados baila con un grupo de baile folklórico.

_____ 3. ¿Qué hace María Inés después de bailar?

c. No, Rosa. Canto en el coro con Luis.

_____ 4. Claudia, tú cantas en el coro con María Inés, ¿verdad?

d. Sí, señor... voy con ellas.

_____ 5. ¿A María Inés le gusta bailar?

e. Está en la Plaza de la Constitución. ¿Vamos allá ahora?

2 Complete Juan José's description of where he and his friends go and what they do after classes with one of the places below.

correo	biblioteca	librería	centro comercial	casa
	gimnasio		cuarto	

Después de clases hoy, voy al **1.** _____ , porque quiero comprar

unas zapatillas nuevas. Mi amiga Diana necesita ir a la **2.** _____ para

hacer la tarea para mañana. Ernesto va primero al **3.** _____. Quiere

comprar unas estampillas (*stamps*). Después va a **4.** _____ porque

necesita organizar su **5.** _____. Susana quiere jugar al voleibol en el

6. _____ con sus amigos. Y Cristóbal va a la

7. _____ porque necesita comprar muchas cosas para las clases.

■ PRIMER PASO

3 Tomás is trying to find someone to shoot baskets with after classes. Complete his conversations with different classmates below with the expressions in the box. Each expression may be used more than once. Does Tomás find someone to play basketball with him?

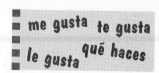

> ■ me gusta te gusta
> ■ le gusta qué haces

TOMÁS   José María, **1.** ¿_____ después de clases?

JOSÉ MARÍA   Juego mucho al basquetbol. Es mi deporte favorito.

TOMÁS   ¿Quieres jugar después de clases hoy?

JOSÉ MARÍA   Necesito hacer la tarea, pero a Carmen **2.** _____ jugar al basquetbol.

TOMÁS   Carmen, **3.** _____ el basquetbol, ¿no?

CARMEN   ¿El basquetbol? Pues no, no **4.** _____ . Me gusta el voleibol.

TOMÁS   ¿El voleibol? Pero a mí no **5.** _____ el voleibol.

CARMEN   Pues habla (*talk*) con David. A él **6.** _____ jugar al basquetbol.

TOMÁS   Oye, David... **7.** ¿_____ el basquetbol?

DAVID   No, pero **8.** _____ nadar. ¿Quieres nadar conmigo hoy después de clases?

TOMÁS   No, gracias. ¡Quiero jugar al basquetbol!

DAVID   Pues... a Luis **9.** _____ practicar los deportes, sobre todo (*especially*) el basquetbol.

TOMÁS   Ah, sí. Y a mí **10.** _____ jugar con Luis. ¡Él juega (*plays*) muy bien! ¡Qué buena idea!

4 Take the role of either Irina or Felipe in the illustrations below. Write a sentence for each picture, saying what you and your friends like and don't like to do.

 Irina

1. _____

 Felipe

2. _____

César

3. _____

¡Ven conmigo! Level 1, Chapter 4

Fernanda

4. _____

Pedro

5. _____

Sarita

6. _____

Juanita

7. _____

5 Write a brief conversation in which you ask a friend what she or he does in some of the places mentioned on an imaginary Friday afternoon. Your friend answers, telling you what she or he does in order from first to last and mentioning one or two things that someone does with her or him.

MODELO   En el colegio...
               Primero, en el colegio, estudio. Luego, en la cafetería...

en el colegio...   en casa...   en el parque...
en la cafetería...   en el centro comercial...

_____
_____
_____
_____
_____
_____
_____
_____
_____
_____

Nombre _____ Clase _____ Fecha _____

6 Look over the vocabulary section on p. 101 of your text, then complete the sentences below with the correct form of the missing verbs. Write the verbs in the correct space in the crossword puzzle.

HORIZONTALES

Guillermo 2. ___ la televisión por la tarde.
Mercedes y yo 4. ___ en la clase de arte.
Nosotros 6. ___ música en mi casa.
Yo siempre 10. ___ a mi hermanito Luis.
Tú 11. ___ con el perro todos los días, ¿verdad?
Javier y Gonzalo 12. ___ la trompeta.
Pilar 13. ___ el carro de su mamá.

VERTICALES

Rebeca 1. ___ en un restaurante italiano.
Yo 3. ___ un refresco con mis amigos.
Después de clases, Manolo 4. ___ en su cuarto.
Mi papá y mi mamá 5. ___ la cena.
Arturo e Isabel 7. ___ en bicicleta en el parque.
Martín nunca 8. ___ la basura.
Carolina 9. ___ el piano.

7 Rosa's friend Héctor always wants to know what's going on. Write out Rosa's answers to Héctor's questions, using the cues in parentheses and following the model below.

MODELO   HÉCTOR   ¿Quién toma un refresco contigo? (Sara y Luis)
            ROSA   **Sara y Luis toman un refresco conmigo.**

1. ¿Quién monta en bicicleta conmigo? (Miguel y yo)

_____

_____

2. ¿Quién trabaja en el restaurante con Susana? (Paco y Lupita)

_____

_____

3. ¿Quién nada con Sebastián y Carlota? (Enrique)

_____

_____

4. ¿Quién mira la tele contigo? (Tú y Miguel)

_____

_____

5. ¿Quién camina en el parque con Germán? (Yo)

_____

¡Ven conmigo! Level 1, Chapter 4

SEGUNDO PASO

8 Franco has just moved to a new town and is writing a letter describing it to his friend Rafael. Complete his letter with the correct form of the verb **estar**.

Querido Rafa,

¿Cómo 1. _____, hombre? Yo 2. _____ muy bien. Me gusta mucho mi nueva ciudad. Mi casa 3. _____ en una zona muy bonita. El Parque de la Constitución 4. _____ muy cerca de la casa. ¡Hay una piscina muy grande en el parque! El colegio 5. _____ lejos. Necesito ir a clases en el autobús o el metro. Pero por suerte, la parada y la estación de metro 6. _____ al lado de mi casa. Mi colegio nuevo se llama Colegio Sarmiento, y 7. _____ en la Plaza de San Juan. Allí hay muchas cosas. Por ejemplo, el cine y la pizzería 8. _____ al lado del colegio. También hay un café cerca.

Bueno, ¿qué tal las clases este año? ¿Cómo 9. _____ Felipe y Marcos? Escríbeme pronto y cuéntame todo.

Un abrazo,
Franco

9 Silvia has never been the neatest person in the world, but this is ridiculous! She can't find anything in her room. Complete Silvia's questions using the drawing of her room, then answer her questions using the prepositions in the box.

MODELO   la mochila
       SILVIA   ¿Dónde está mi mochila?
          TÚ   **Está debajo de la cama.**

encima de	debajo de
al lado de	cerca de

1. ¡Ay, pero soy un desastre! ¿Dónde _____ mis zapatillas?

_____

_____

2. Tengo clase. ¿_____ están mis libros?

_____

_____

3. ¡Mi tarea! ¿_____?

_____

_____

4. ¡El dinero! ¿Dónde está el dinero?

_____

_____

5. Llamamos *(Let's call)* a Rafael. ¿Pero dónde está el teléfono?

_____

_____

6. Quiero tocar la guitarra. ¿Pero dónde está?

_____

_____

7. ¿Dónde está el diccionario?

_____

_____

8. Necesito hacer la tarea de matemáticas. ¿Dónde está la calculadora?

_____

_____

9. Mmmm. ¿Dónde está la pizza?

_____

_____

10 You know that you don't use subject pronouns in Spanish as often as in English, but you still need to know them and understand what pronoun to use with whom. Look over the **Gramática** section on p. 109 of your textbook, then answer the questions below.

What subject pronoun should you use to talk **to** the following people?

1. tu amiga Maripili

 _____

3. tu amigo Rodolfo

 _____

2. la profesora Benavides

 _____

4. tus amigos españoles, Concha y Manolo

  _____

What subject pronoun should you use to talk **about** the following people?

5. el Sr. Durán, director del colegio

 _____

7. tus amigas Margarita y Susana

 _____

6. tu amigo Bernardo

 _____

8. tú y tu amigo Sergio

 _____

TERCER PASO

11 Carolina and Leonora are talking about everyone's plans for the weekend. Read through their conversation and fill in the blanks with the correct form of **ir**.

CAROLINA   Oye, Leonora, ¿adónde _____ tú el sábado?

LEONORA   ¿Yo? Bueno, por la mañana _____ a la piscina para nadar. Marián _____ conmigo. ¿Quieres ir con nosotras? Nosotras vamos allá a las doce.

CAROLINA   Yo _____ al cine con Francisco a las doce, pero si tú y Marián _____ a la piscina más tarde, a las cuatro...

LEONORA   Ay, chica, lo siento, pero no puedo (*I'm sorry, but I can't*). Mi famila y yo _____ a un concierto de jazz. Marián _____ con nosotros. ¿Quieres ir también?

CAROLINA   Bueno, a mí me gusta el jazz. ¿A qué hora _____ ustedes?

LEONORA   _____ a las cuatro y media. Entonces, ven a mi casa a las cuatro si quieres ir. ¿Está bien?

CAROLINA   Perfecto, hasta luego.

12 Carlos and his friends are always going one place or another. But Carlos is sick today. Put the following information from his phone messages together to ask and tell where everyone's going and what they're going to do today. Follow the model.

MODELO   Marta / gimnasio / 3:30 / jugar al voleibol
              ¿Adónde va Marta?
              Marta va al gimnasio a las tres y media para jugar al voleibol.

1. Joaquín / parque / 4:00 / caminar con los perros de la Sra. Sánchez

   ¿_____?

   _____

2. José y Lalo / casa de Marcos / 5:30 / hacer la tarea

   ¿_____?

   _____

3. Claudia, Leti y Néstor / cine / 7:00

   ¿_____?

   _____

4. Eugenia, Iván y tú / restaurante / tomar un refresco

   ¿_____?

   _____

5. tú / parque / ahora / montar en bicicleta

   ¿_____?

   _____

13 Which day or days of the week do you associate with the following things or activities? Write the day or days you associate with each, then explain why.

MODELO   lavar el carro
                    los domingos: En mi casa, siempre lavamos el carro los domingos.

1. los deportes _____

   _____

2. ir a un restaurante _____

   _____

3. los bailes _____

   _____

4. mirar la televisión _____

   _____

5. lavar la ropa _____

   _____

6. organizar mi cuarto _____

   _____

7. ir al centro comercial _____

   _____

8. descansar _____

   _____

9. trabajar _____

   _____

14 What are your favorite and least favorite days of the week? Explain why you like or don't like each of these days, as in the **modelo**.

MODELO   los martes, los domingos
                    Me gustan los martes...
                    No me gustan los domingos...

_____

_____

_____

_____

_____

15 It's getting close to the holidays and your calendar is filling up fast! To keep track of everything, make an agenda for the coming week. For each day, list one thing you want or need to do, and a place you will go. Use the expressions **necesito** + infinitive, **quiero** + infinitive, and **voy a...** .

MODELO   **El lunes necesito estudiar. Voy al cine con Diego.**

AGENDA PARA LA SEMANA QUE VIENE
lunes
martes
miércoles
jueves
viernes

16 Imagine that Esteban, a friend of yours from Mexico, is coming to visit you in a few weeks. He'll come on a Saturday and leave the following Wednesday. Write him a postcard telling him your plans for the two of you. For each day, mention one place the two of you will go, and what you'll do there. Remember to ask Esteban if he likes the activities and places you've included in your plans!

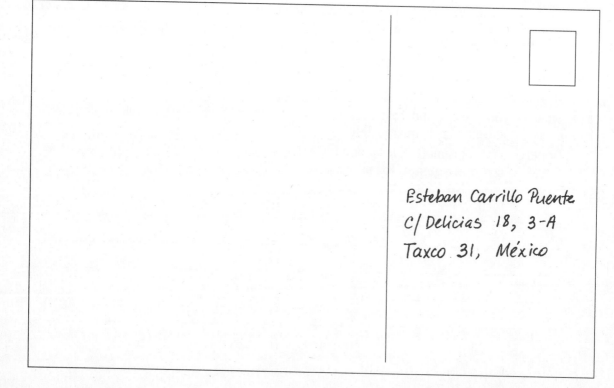

Esteban Carrillo Puente
C/ Delicias 18, 3-A
Taxco 31, México

¡Ven conmigo! Level 1, Chapter 4

■ VAMOS A LEER

17 To the right is part of a brochure advertising different activities offered at the YMCA sports club in Buenos Aires, Argentina. Look over the page and answer the following questions.

a. The ad lists four main topics. Look over what's listed under each of these topics, then match each topic to its English equivalent below.

_____ 1. deportes

_____ 2. actividades socio-culturales

_____ 3. instalaciones

_____ 4. gimnasia

   a. *facilities*
   b. *gymnastics*
   c. *sports*
   d. *social and cultural activities*

b. Can you figure out which sports go on in which part of the Buenos Aires YMCA? Match up each **deporte** with its correct **instalación**.

_____ 1. natación

_____ 2. pelota a mano

_____ 3. aerobismo

_____ 4. basquetbol y voleibol

   a. pista aeróbica

   b. gimnasios cerrados

   c. piletas climatizadas

   d. canchas de pelota a mano

ACJ. A 5 minutos de la oficina.

GIMNASIA:
- Mantenimiento.
- Aero-local.
- Step training.
- Low impact.
- Body scultura.
- Cross training.
- Yoga.
- Streching.
- Rehabilitación cardiovascular.
- Aquaerobic.
- Relax time.
- Tai chi chuan.

ACTIVIDADES SOCIO CULTURALES:
- Ajedrez.
- Fotografía.
- Tango.
- Folklore.
- Teatro.
- Salidas y excurciones.
- Campamentos.

DEPORTES:
- Natación.
- Papi-fútbol.
- Básquetbol.
- Vóleibol.
- Racquet-ball.
- Pelota mano.
- Karate.
- Aerobismo.
- Buceo.

INSTALACIONES:
- Piletas climatizadas.
- Gimnasios cerrados.
- Solarium.
- Gimnasio de pesas y complementos.
- Pista aeróbica.
- Baño sauna.
- Canchas de pelota a mano.
- Restaurant y confitería.

ASOCIACION CRISTIANA DE JOVENES (YMCA)

Informes planta baja de lunes a viernes de 9 a 20 hs. y sábados de 9 a 12 hs.
Reconquista 439 - 311-4785/86/87 313-8953/8938

---

c. Now look more carefully at the listings under **Gimnasia**, **Deportes**, and **Actividades**. Many of the words are cognates, so you should see words you recognize and understand. Make a list below of sports and activities offered at the Buenos Aires YMCA that you like.

_____

_____

_____

_____

_____

■ CULTURA

18 Decide if the following statements were probably made by **a)** a student in the United States, **b)** a student in a Spanish-speaking country, or **c)** both.

_____ 1. A las cuatro, voy a la reunión (*meeting*) del Club de drama.

_____ 2. Este año, quiero participar en el club de computadoras de mi colegio. ¡Me gustan mucho los videojuegos!

_____ 3. Los domingos, siempre vamos a la casa de mis abuelos o caminamos en el parque.

_____ 4. Después de clases, por lo general voy a casa para hacer la tarea para mañana.

_____ 5. Hoy tengo entrenamiento (*practice*) de karate. Mi colegio tiene un equipo de karate excelente.

_____ 6. Después de clases, a veces tomo un refresco con unos amigos en el café, o caminamos en el parque.

_____ 7. Esta semana mi equipo de fútbol va a jugar contra el equipo de Taxco. ¡Va a ser un partido padrísimo!

19 Your class has just received a letter from the **Colegio Reforma** in Cuernavaca, Mexico. They have a lot of questions about life and school in the U.S. You've been assigned to answer the questions given below. Write a short paragraph in Spanish answering the questions below.

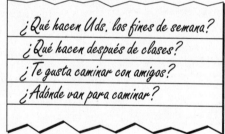

¿Qué hacen Uds. los fines de semana?
¿Qué hacen después de clases?
¿Te gusta caminar con amigos?
¿Adónde van para caminar?

_____

_____

_____

_____

_____

_____

_____

_____

CAPÍTULO 5

5

El ritmo de la vida

■ DE ANTEMANO

1 Armando is a new student at Seminole High School in Miami. First read the letter he wrote to his cousin Yolanda in Panama about his new home and new routine, then answer the questions below.

Miami, 8 de noviembre

Querida Yolanda,

¿Cómo estás? Yo, muy bien. Aquí el ritmo de la vida es increíble. Hay muchísimas cosas que hacer en los ratos libres. Durante la semana, estoy muy ocupado. Los lunes y los jueves tengo la clase de artes marciales. Me gustan mucho el karate y el tae-kwon-do. Los martes tenemos la reunión del Club de arte de mi colegio. ¡Este año quiero ser presidente del club! Los miércoles y los viernes toco la batería en la banda del colegio. Tocamos en los partidos de fútbol todos los viernes por la noche. Los sábados por la noche, a veces vamos a una discoteca para bailar, o a una fiesta en casa de amigos. Los domingos, voy con mamá y papá a comer en un restaurante cubano. Pienso que la comida cubana es fantástica... a mis padres les gusta mucho también.

Bueno, escríbeme y cuéntame cómo están todos. Un fuerte abrazo para ti y para mis tíos.

Con cariño,
Armando

Look at Armando's schedule. Based on what he wrote in his letter, decide if all of the information is accurate. Check **sí** if it is correct. Check **no** if it is not. For the items that are not correct, fill in the calendar with the correct information.

		sí	no
lunes	*clase de artes marciales*		
martes	*reunión del Club de español*		
miércoles	*toca la batería con la orquesta*		
jueves	*clase de arte*		
viernes	*toca la batería con la banda*		
sábado	*va a la discoteca*		
domingo	*va a un restaurante chino*		

■ PRIMER PASO

2 Xóchitl hasn't seen her grandmother for a while. Read the questions her **abuela** (*grandmother*) asks her, then write Xóchitl's responses, using the cues in parentheses. Follow the model.

MODELO   Mi hija, ¡estás muy delgada! ¿No desayunas? (siempre)
             Sí, abuela, siempre desayuno.

1. ¡Xóchitl! ¿Nunca organizas tu cuarto? ¡Es un desastre! (a veces)

   _____

2. Xóchitl, ¿todavía tocas el piano? Tócame (*Play me*) algo de Beethoven. (nunca)

   _____

3. Xóchitl, ¿con qué frecuencia ayudas en casa? (todos los días)

   _____

4. Xóchitl, ¿vas al cine con tus amigos durante la semana? (sólo cuando no tengo tarea)

   _____

3 Using the cues provided, write a true statement that each person might make using **siempre** or **no (nunca)**. Base your answers on what you know and on the cultural information you learned so far.

MODELO   **Alma, Lawrence, Kansas:** tener nueve clases al día
             Aquí nunca tenemos nueve clases al día.

1. **Juan, New York, New York:** regresar a casa a las doce del día para el almuerzo.

   _____

   _____

2. **Conchita, Oaxaca, México:** En el colegio, tener por lo menos (*at least*) ocho asignaturas.

   _____

   _____

3. **Marcos, Valencia, España:** Para ir a la casa de un amigo, tomar el autobús.

   _____

   _____

4. **Lourdes, San Ysidro, California:** En mi colegio, haber clases después de las tres y media de la tarde.

   _____

   _____

4 What's it like to be a millionaire at sixteen? Read this interview between **Música y más** magazine and Adrián, a teenage star. Then respond to the statements that follow with **cierto** or **falso**. Correct the false statements.

Música y más entrevista a... *Adrián Sandoval*

M y m Seguro, Adrián, que no tienes tiempo para muchas cosas...

Adrián Bueno, ¡soy más normal de lo que piensas! (*I'm more normal than you think!*) Siempre tengo tiempo para mis amigos.

M y m Tienes una vida social muy ocupada (*a very busy social life*), ¿verdad?

Adrián A veces necesito cantar en conciertos o en programas de televisión. Pero, generalmente (*usually*), durante la semana estoy en casa.

M y m ¿Y cómo es un día típico?

Adrián Bueno, siempre desayuno. Después voy al colegio.

M y m ¡Qué bien! Y después del colegio, ¿qué haces?

Adrián A ver, a veces necesito trabajar en el estudio. Y necesito hacer la tarea todos los días.

M y m ¿Y los fines de semana?

Adrián Bueno, muchas veces no hago nada. Pero a veces me gusta ir con amigos a un restaurante o al cine, pero sólo cuando no tengo mucha tarea.

M y m Ya eres millonario, ¿no? ¿Y todavía ayudas en casa?

Adrián ¡Siempre! Muchas veces cuido a mis hermanos, y a veces aun (*even*) preparo la comida.

M y m ¿Y qué tal la comida que preparas?

Adrián ¡Horrible! ¡Guácala! (*Yuck!*)

---

1. Adrián no necesita cantar en conciertos todos los días.

   _____

2. Muchas veces Adrián no desayuna porque está atrasado.

   _____

3. Adrián siempre hace muchas cosas los fines de semana.

   _____

4. Durante la semana va con amigos a un restaurante o al cine.

   _____

5. Adrián siempre prepara la comida.

   _____

5 Make a list in Spanish of four things you never do, and explain why you never do them. Look at the vocabulary list for Chapter 5 if you need some ideas.

MODELO   Nunca voy a los partidos de fútbol del colegio porque siempre trabajo los sábados por la mañana en el supermercado.

_____

_____

_____

_____

_____

6 Who are your favorite people? Answer the questions below, explaining why each person or group of people is your favorite.

MODELO   ¿Quién es tu persona favorita?
Mi "persona" favorita es mi perro Sam. No es una persona, pero es muy simpático y cómico.

1. ¿Quién es tu profesora favorita? _____
   _____

2. ¿Quién es tu cantante (*singer*) favorito? _____
   _____

3. ¿Quién es tu mejor amigo o amiga? _____
   _____

4. ¿Quiénes son tus atletas favoritos? _____

7 What kind of life do you lead? Is it too busy, too disorganized, or just right? Take the following magazine poll to analyze your lifestyle. Answer each question based on what's true for you. Keep track of how many **a.**, **b.** and **c.** answers you've circled, and then read the article's description of your personality and lifestyle. Is it correct?

¿Te gusta el ritmo de tu vida?

1. ¿Con qué frecuencia haces la tarea?
  a. siempre
  b. a veces
  c. nunca

2. ¿Con qué frecuencia descansas o duermes la siesta (*do you take a nap*)?
  a. nunca o casi nunca
  b. a veces
  c. todos los días

3. ¿Con qué frecuencia organizas tu cuarto?
  a. todos los días
  b. sólo cuando sea (*it's*) necesario
  c. nunca

4. ¿Con qué frecuencia vas al cine con tus amigos?
  a. nunca
  b. a veces
  c. todos los días

5. ¿Con qué frecuencia lavas los platos?
  a. todos los días
  b. a veces
  c. nunca

6. ¿Con qué frecuencia miras la televisión?
  a. nunca
  b. sólo a veces, para mirar mis programas favoritos
  c. siempre

7. ¿Con qué frecuencia sacas la basura?
  a. siempre
  b. a veces
  c. nunca

8. ¿Con qué frecuencia practicas un deporte?
  a. nunca
  b. a veces
  c. todos los días

Análisis:

a.—Si la mayoría (*most*) de tus respuestas son **a.**, entonces trabajas mucho—¡y es un problema! Tienes un ritmo de vida muy acelerado y complicado. Necesitas tomar las cosas con más tranquilidad. Necesitas descansar más y hacer cosas divertidas en tus ratos libres.

b.—Si la mayoría de tus respuestas son **b.**, está bien. Eres una persona equilibrada. En tu vida hay un balance entre el trabajo, las responsabilidades y los ratos libres. Trabajas, pero también descansas.

c.—Si la mayoría de tus respuestas son **c.**, entonces descansas mucho—¡y es un problema! Tienes un ritmo de vida desorganizado. Necesitas ser más responsable y organizado en tu trabajo o en tus estudios. Recuerda que en la vida es importante tener un balance entre el descanso y el trabajo.

■ SEGUNDO PASO

8 Next year you will be an exchange student in Montevideo. Below is a letter from Clara, your host student, about what she and her friends like to do in their spare time. Read Clara's letter and complete it with the correct words or phrases from the box.

les	nos	te
a ellos		le
me	a ellos	

Querido amigo,

¡Hola! Me llamo Clara Serrano, y soy de Montevideo, Uruguay. A mí 1. _____ gustan muchas cosas: montar en bicicleta en el parque, comer pizza en el centro y pasar el rato con mis amigos. Después de clases, a nosotros 2. _____ gusta ir al cine. A mi amigo Leonardo 3. _____ gustan las películas de aventuras. Mis amigas Carmen y Rebeca son simpáticas. 4. _____ les gustan las películas de ciencia-ficción. Y qué curiosos son mis amigos Horacio y Abel. 5. _____ les gustan mucho las películas de horror. Vamos al cine dos veces por semana. A mí 6. _____ gusta ir por la tarde, pero a mis amigos 7. _____ gusta ir por la noche. ¿A ti 8. _____ gusta ir al cine? ¿Qué películas 9. _____ gustan?

9 For each of the drawings below, write a sentence explaining what the people pictured like, or don't like, to do. Then say how often they do the activities shown.

Marta y Susana

Isabel y Bingo

Joaquín y Laura

David y Micaela

1. _____

_____

2. _____

_____

3. _____

_____

4. _____

_____

10

Imagine that you have a twin brother named Silvio. You both like to do many of the same things. Look at the lists of favorite activities for you and your twin. If only one of you likes an activity, write a sentence saying which one of you likes it. If you both like an activity, write a sentence saying that you like to do that activity together.

Yo	Silvio
esquiar	pescar
acampar	acampar
bucear	hacer ejercicio
correr por la playa	correr por la playa
hacer ejercicio	bucear

1. _____

2. _____

3. _____

4. _____

5. _____

6. _____

11

The sentences below describe what some students and teachers at Seminole High School do in their free time. Complete the sentences with the correct forms of the verbs in parentheses, then check your answers by filling in the crossword puzzle with the missing words.

Horizontales

2. En la clase de literatura, nosotros ____ muchas novelas. (leer)
5. Todos los estudiantes ____ la reunión a las tres y media. (asistir a)
7. Martín y yo ____ un concierto este sábado. (asistir a)
9. Yo ____ una carta a mi amigo en La Habana todos los martes. (escribir)
10. Yo siempre ____ un sándwich en el almuerzo. (comer)
12. Santiago y Teresa ____ cartas cuando tienen tiempo. (escribir)
13. Nosotros ____ tacos en la cafetería del colegio los miércoles. (comer)

Verticales

1. Fátima y yo ____ una carta de España todos los sábados. (recibir)
2. Por la mañana, yo ____ el periódico en casa (leer).
3. Ricardo, ¿cuándo ____ la tarea, por la tarde o por la noche? (hacer)
4. ¿Qué ____ Elena después de clases? (hacer)
6. En la clase de historia, nosotros ____ composiciones. (escribir)
8. Nosotros siempre ____ agua después de correr. (beber)
10. El Sr. Guzmán y su perro Bobby ____ en el parque los fines de semana. (correr)
11. Germán y Lola ____ sus libros de texto en el autobús. (leer)

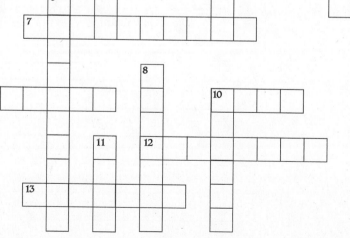

12 The planet Xargon has sent a team of investigators to find out about our planet and its inhabitants. You have been chosen to interpret the Xargonians' interviews for a Spanish-speaking audience. First write out the Xargonians' questions (items 1, 3, and 5). Then write what the earthlings answered, using expressions from the box below.

> todos los días   sólo cuando...   muchas veces
> durante...   a veces   por la mañana   siempre
> por la noche   nunca   por la tarde

1. (The Xargonians want to know how often earthlings go to school.)

   _____

   _____

2. _____

   _____

3. (The Xargonians want to know what students do after class.)

   _____

   _____

4. _____

   _____

5. (The Xargonians want to know if students like to talk on the phone and how often.)

   _____

   _____

6. _____

   _____

CAPÍTULO 5 Segundo paso

Nombre _____ Clase _____ Fecha _____

■ TERCER PASO

13 By now you've learned how to talk about what day, month, and season it is in Spanish. Unscramble the words whose definitions appear below. If you unscramble each word correctly, you will find a message in the shaded vertical column.

MODELO __m_ __a_ __r_ __z_ __o__   (El mes después de febrero)
         r   m   a   o   z

1. __ __ __ __ __ __ __ __ __   El día entre (*between*) el martes y el jueves.
    e l m c é i o r s

2. __ __ __ __ __ __ __   El mes antes de noviembre.
       c r b e u o t

3. __ __ __ __ __ __   El día después del viernes.
       b s d á a o

4. __ __ __ __ __   El mes entre marzo y mayo.
    i l b r a

5. __ __ __ __ __   La estación antes del otoño.
       a v r o n e

6. __ __ __ __ __ __   El día después del lunes.
    s m e t r a

7. __ __ __ __ __   El día después del domingo.
       e l n s u

8. __ __ __ __ __ __ __ __   La estación antes del verano.
    e r p a v i m a r

9. __ __ __ __ __   La palabra en español para *date*.
       h a f c e

10. __ __ __ __ __ __ __ __   La estación antes de la primavera.
    v o n r i i e n

11. __ __ __ __ __ __ __ __ __   El mes después de noviembre.
       e r d m c b e i i

12. __ __ __   El día antes de mañana.
    y h o

13. __ __ __ __ __ __   El mes entre julio y septiembre.
    t a o g o s

14 Your pen pal Rosario from Perú wants to know about some U.S. holidays. Tell Rosario in what month the following special days fall this year.

1. El Día de la Independencia _____

2. El Día de Acción de Gracias (*Thanksgiving*) _____

3. El primer día del verano _____

4. El Día de San Valentín _____

5. El Año Nuevo _____

6. Tu cumpleaños (*birthday*) _____

¡Ven conmigo! Level 1, Chapter 5

HRW material copyrighted under notice appearing earlier in this work.

15 It's easy to forget which season some months fall in! Read Javier's and Miguel's conversation, filling in the blanks with the correct seasons and months.

JAVIER Oye, Miguel, ¿cuál es tu estación favorita? La primavera, ¿verdad?

MIGUEL ¡Ya sabes que me gusta más el verano! Los meses de _____,

_____, y _____, cuando hace calor y voy a la piscina a

nadar todos los días.

JAVIER Y el mes de septiembre, también, ¿no?

MIGUEL No, hombre. Septiembre es un mes de _____.

JAVIER Ah, sí, tienes razón *(you're right)*. Con _____ y _____.

MIGUEL Y no te olvides de *(don't forget about)* diciembre.

JAVIER No, diciembre está en _____. También los meses de _____

y _____.

MIGUEL Y, por fin, _____, _____ y _____ son meses de

_____.

16 For each of the illustrations below, write what season it is and what the weather is usually like where you live.

 1. octubre _____

_____

 2. junio _____

_____

 3. abril _____

_____

 4. enero _____

_____

 5. marzo _____

_____

 6. julio _____

_____

17 The weather can have a big effect on our daily activities. Look at the drawings of people below, and write one or two sentences describing what the people shown are doing or where they're going, and what the weather is like.

1. Elena y Sergio   2. El Sr. Jiménez   3. Susanita y Benjamín   4. Doña Blanca

1. _____

   _____

2. _____

   _____

3. _____

   _____

4. _____

   _____

18 What's your favorite time of year? Write a short paragraph of about eight lines in which you tell what season you like best and why. What's the weather like? What kinds of things do you and your friends like to do then?

_____

_____

_____

_____

_____

_____

_____

_____

█ VAMOS A LEER

19 Read the two comic strips, then answer the questions below.

me molesta = *bothers me*   **humedad** = *humidity*   **salta** = *jump out*

tontas = *stupid*   **asoleado** = *sunny*   **regadera** = *watering can*
influir sobre sus mentes = *to play with their minds*

a. Check your comprehension by answering the following questions.

1. Why isn't Hobbes (the tiger) going to like the end of his wagon ride? _____

    _____

2. How do you think Hobbes would describe Calvin in the last frame of the second strip?
    Write a caption in Spanish to express what he thinks of Calvin.

    _____

    _____

b. Read the following descriptions of Calvin and Hobbes and decide if they are accurate. If
so, circle **sí**. If not, circle **no**. Then correct all of the information that is not accurate.

1. Calvin es alto, moreno y antipático.   sí   no

2. A Calvin no le gusta jugar.   sí   no

3. Hobbes es cómico, inteligente y simpático.   sí   no

4. A Calvin y Hobbes les gusta pasar el rato juntos. sí   no

¡Ven conmigo! Level 1, Chapter 5   Practice and Activity Book **59**

HRW material copyrighted under notice appearing earlier in this work.

■ CULTURA

20 Based upon what you've learned about Spanish-speaking young people, correct the following statements if they are false.

1. It's fairly common for young people in Spain or Latin America to have their own cars.

   _____

2. Spanish-speaking young people often will make plans to meet friends in a park, a café or some other public place.

   _____

3. The streets of the average town or city in a Spanish-speaking country will most likely be deserted after sundown.

   _____

4. Young people in the Spanish-speaking world often tend to socialize in groups.

   _____

21 Imagine that you're a travel agent, specializing in trips to Latin America. What kind of clothing would you advise your customers to take with them if they're going to . . .? Explain briefly what the weather is like in each case.

1. make a trip to Argentina in December and January

   _____

   _____

2. travel to southern Chile in mid-July

   _____

   _____

3. take a tour of the Andean region of Ecuador in May

   _____

   _____

22 Imagine that you're going to spend the month of January in Buenos Aires, Argentina. Through an exchange program, you'll be living with an Argentine family with two kids your age. In this chapter you've read about Spanish-speaking young people and about the climate in southern South America. Based on what you've learned in this chapter, what might you expect to see and experience with your host family in Buenos Aires?

_____

_____

_____

_____

_____

¡Ven conmigo! Level 1, Chapter 5

■ DE ANTEMANO

1 When Raquel shows Armando her family's photo album, he asks some questions about her family. Can you match Armando's questions with Raquel's answers?

Armando

_____ 1. ¿De dónde es tu tía Luisa?

_____ 2. ¿Dónde vive tu hermano Carlos ahora?

_____ 3. A Uds. les gusta la música, ¿verdad?

_____ 4. ¿Qué hacen Uds. durante las vacaciones de Navidad?

_____ 5. ¿Sales mucho con tus hermanos?

Raquel

a. Para Navidades, vamos a Tampa y visitamos a mis tíos y mis abuelos que viven allí.

b. Ella es de Cuba, como mis padres.

c. Sí, salgo con ellos bastante. Muchas veces voy con mis hermanos al cine o al centro comercial. ¡A veces salimos a bailar!

d. ¡Muchísimo! Todos tocamos por lo menos un instrumento musical.

e. Ahora él vive en Gainesville. Estudia en la Universidad de Florida.

2 Look at the family portraits and circle the description that best matches each portrait.

1.

a. Ésta es mi familia: mis padres, mi hermano, mi hermana y mi abuela.

b. Aquí estamos todos: mi madre, mi padre, mi hermano y yo.

c. Aquí ves a mi familia: mi padre, mi madre, mi hermana, nuestro perro y yo.

2.

a. Éstos son mis hermanos.

b. En esta foto estamos todos: mi padre, mi madre y yo.

c. Éstos son mis abuelos.

3.

a. Éstos son mis padres.

b. Ésta es mi familia: mis padres, mis dos hermanos menores y yo.

c. Ésta es mi familia: mis padres, mis dos primos y mi abuelo.

PRIMER PASO

3 Look over the **Vocabulario** on p. 153 of your textbook, then complete the crossword puzzle.

Horizontales

5. El padre de tu padre
8. El hijo de tu madre y tu padrastro
10. Lo contrario de hermano
12. La hermana de tu padre
13. Los hijos de tu tío
14. La madre de tu padre
15. Las hijas de tus tíos

Verticales

1. El hermano de tu madre
2. Lo contrario de padre
3. La hija de tu madrastra o tu padrastro
4. Lo contrario de esposa
6. El hijo de tu abuelo y el esposo de tu madre
7. El esposo de tu madre, pero que no es tu verdadero padre
9. La esposa de tu padre, pero que no es tu verdadera madre
10. Tu padre es el ___ de tu abuela paterna
11. Tu madre es la ___ de tu abuelo materno

4 Guillermo Montes has invited Lupe to his house for a family party. She's never met any of his family before, and as his relatives come into the living room, Guillermo points out everyone to Lupe. Complete his sentences with **éste**, **ésta**, **éstos**, or **éstas**.

1. _____ son mis primas, Rosita y Carmen. Son estudiantes en la Universidad de Florida. Y 2. _____ es mi abuelita. Ella vive con nosotros. 3. _____ son mis hermanitos, Alfonso y Carlitos. Son super-pesados (*pains*). 4. _____ es mi madre. A ella le gustan mucho estas fiestas grandes. 5. _____ son mis tíos, Isabel y Armando. Ellos viven en Orlando. 6. _____ es mi hermana mayor, Gloria... ¡ y 7. _____ es mi sobrinito, Javier! Sólo tiene seis meses, pero ya sé que es muy inteligente. Y 8. _____ es mi padre. A él le gustan las fiestas, pero prefiere (*he prefers*) leer el periódico.

¡Ven conmigo! Level 1, Chapter 6

5 Imagine that you're having a conversation with Pilar Guzmán Franco about her family. Using her family tree and the cues provided, write your questions and Pilar's answers.

1. TÚ (Ask how many people there are in Pilar's family.)

   _____

   _____

María Fuentes de Guzmán   Francisco Guzmán

2. PILAR _____

   _____

Elena Franco de Guzmán   Rolando Guzmán Fuentes   Elisa Guzmán Fuentes de García   Lorenzo García

3. TÚ (Ask what Pilar's parents are like.)

   _____

4. PILAR _____

   _____

Pilar Guzmán Franco   Fernando Guzmán Franco   Fabiola Guzmán Franco   Ana García Guzmán   Humberto García Guzmán

Tiburón, el pez   Simba

5. TÚ (Ask what Pilar's grandparents' names are.)

   _____

6. PILAR _____

   _____

7. TÚ (Ask if Pilar and her brother have any pets [**animales domésticos**].)

   _____

8. PILAR _____

   _____

6 The words **su** and **sus** can be confusing, because they mean so many different things: *your, his, her, their*. In a conversation, though, context will make the meaning of these words clear. How many meanings can the expressions below have? Circle all of the English expressions that match each Spanish one. Some expressions may have more than one match.

MODELO   su hijo
              (a.) el hijo de él   **b.** los hijos de ella   (c.) el hijo de Uds.

1. su casa
   a. la casa de ella   **b.** la casa de Uds.   **c.** las casas de Ud.
2. sus abuelos
   a. la abuela de ellos   **b.** los abuelos de Ud.   **c.** los abuelos de Uds.
3. su hermano
   a. el hermano de él   **b.** los hermanos de ellos   **c.** el hermano de Uds.
4. su madrastra
   a. la madrastra de nosotros   **b.** la madrastra de María   **c.** la madrastra de Uds.
5. sus padres
   a. los padres de Uds.   **b.** el padre de ellas   **c.** los padres de nosotras
6. su familia
   a. la familia de Pedro y Juan   **b.** la familia de Uds.   **c.** la familia de Ud.
7. sus primos
   a. los primos de nosotros   **b.** el primo de ellas   **c.** los primos de Lupe
8. sus tíos
   a. los tíos de Pilar   **b.** los tíos de ella   **c.** los tíos de Uds.

7 Complete Carmen's description of her family with the corrrect possessive adjectives.

¡Hola! Me llamo Carmen Iriarte y soy de Nueva York. Te quiero describir a **1.** _____ *(my)* familia. **2.** _____ *(Our)* familia es un poco complicada—somos muy internacionales. **3.** _____ *(My)* madre se llama Ana y es de Argentina originalmente. Ahora vive aquí en Nueva York. **4.** _____ *(Her)* hermano Roberto vive aquí también. **5.** _____ *(His)* esposa es de Irlanda. Se llama Maureen. **6.** _____ *(Their)* dos hijitos se llaman Brian y Sara. Me encanta ir a la casa de **7.** _____ *(my)* tíos Roberto y Maureen y jugar con **8.** _____ *(my)* dos sobrinitos. **9.** _____ *(their)* videojuegos son super-divertidos.

10. _____ *(My)* padres están divorciados. **11.** _____ *(My)* padre Antonio es español. Vive ahora en España con **12.** _____ *(his)* segunda esposa, Marián. **13.** _____ *(their)* casa está en Sevilla. Marián es muy cariñosa. **14.** _____ *(Her)* hijo Alfonso es **15.** _____ *(my)* hermanastro. Somos muy buenos amigos. Él quiere aprender inglés. Entonces, el año que viene, Alfonso va a vivir en **16.** _____ *(our)* apartamento en Nueva York y estudiar aquí. ¡Y yo voy a Sevilla a vivir en **17.** _____ *(his)* piso y estudiar en **18.** _____ *(his)* colegio. Qué complicado, ¿verdad?

8 Juan and Daniela Barrón are brother and sister. The pictures below are of their family. Take the role of either Juan or Daniela. First think of a name for each member of the family, and label him or her accordingly (Juan and Daniela are already labeled for you.) Also say how he or she is related to you. Then write a short paragraph answering the following questions.

¿Cuántas personas hay en tu familia? ¿Cómo es tu familia? ¿Cuántas personas viven en tu casa? ¿Tienen un animal doméstico? ¿Quiénes son las personas en estas fotos?

_____

_____

_____

_____

_____

■ SEGUNDO PASO

9 Look at the Guzmán family tree in Activity 5. Answer the following questions about members of Pilar's family, using the what you've learned in Chapter 6 as well as any other words you know. Use your imagination to describe them.

1. ¿Cómo es Humberto?¿De qué color es su pelo? ¿De qué color son sus ojos? ¿Cuántos años tiene?

_____

_____

2. ¿Cómo es María? ¿De qué color es su pelo? ¿Cuántos años tiene?

_____

_____

3. ¿Cómo es la abuela de Pilar? ¿De qué color es su pelo? ¿Cuántos años tiene?

_____

_____

4. ¿Cómo es Simba? ¿De qué color es su pelo?

_____

_____

10 How would you describe your best friend? Think of someone you're close to, either a family member or a friend, and write five to six sentences describing that person. Use the adjectives on pp. 158 and 159 of your textbook, as well as any others you've learned. Below are some other words you can use. Many of them are cognates.

comprensivo(a) *understanding*	**chismoso(a)** *gossipy*	**tener...años**
honrado(a) *honest*	**(im)paciente** *(im)patient*	**vivir en...**
(in)maduro(a) *(im)mature*	**irresponsable** *irresponsible*	**le gusta...**
sincero(a) *sincere*	**valiente** *brave*	

_____

_____

_____

_____

_____

_____

_____

11 Combine elements from the columns to write four original sentences telling how often these people do the activities listed. Use the "personal **a**" as appropriate.

MODELO   **Mis padres no visitan a sus primos nunca.**

yo	llamar (a)	mis abuelos	nunca
mis padres	visitar (a)	un museo	siempre
el/la profesor(a)	querer conocer (a)	sus primos	con frecuencia

1. _____

2. _____

3. _____

4. _____

12 Look over this page from Andrés Benavente's address book. Then, using the cues provided, ask him for some information about his family.

1. what his family is like

   _____

   _____

2. what he and his family do together on weekends

   _____

   _____

3. where the people in his family live

   _____

   _____

Now write Andrés's answers to your questions. Mention at least two things in item 5. In item 6, write where Andrés would say at least four members of his family live, including himself. Use your imagination!

4. _____

   _____

5. _____

   _____

6. _____

   _____

```
Jacobo Benavente Dávila
C.P. #278
Arecibo 00613
PUERTO RICO
─────────────────────────
Ana María Benavente
P.O. Box 8733
University of Florida
Gainesville, FL  31559
(en Miami: 3225 Buena
Vista Avenue
Miami, FL  35921)
─────────────────────────
Benigno Benavente Rubio y
Alma Ybarra de Benavente
C/ Palomar 92, 3
San Juan 00231
PUERTO RICO
─────────────────────────
Martín Berenger
Carrer dels Angels, 47, 6A
Barcelona  54022
ESPAÑA
─────────────────────────
Lidia Calero
11 Cra. 5 #6-64 B
Cartagena
COLOMBIA
─────────────────────────
Alejandro Galdós Sobejano
C/ Arteaga 1483
Colonia Centro, Nuevo
Laredo
Tamaulipas MEXICO
─────────────────────────
Carolina Irizarri de la
Vega
C/ 15 de septiembre, 42
Metapán, Sta. Ana
EL SALVADOR
─────────────────────────
Néstor Muñoz Arévalo
Avda. 13, #59, 7B
Maracaibo VENEZUELA
```

13 Mercedes and Laura are tennis partners and friends. Below are their calendars for the next week. Read them through, then answer the questions below. Do Mercedes and Laura have anything in common besides tennis?

MODELO   ¿Cuándo sale Mercedes con su tía Julia? ¿Qué hacen?
Mercedes sale con su tía Julia el viernes a la una. Van al centro comercial.

EL HORARIO DE MERCEDES

lunes 16	martes 17	miércoles 18	jueves 19	viernes 20	sábado 21	domingo 22
Laura— tenis 4:00	Mamá— visitar al tío Rubén 3:30	Miguel— 5:00 biblioteca para el examen de historia	Laura— tenis 4:00	Tía Julia— 1:00, al centro comercial Mamá y papá— cumpleaños de Abuelo	Roberto— cine 4:30 ♥	Abuela— misa 10:30

EL HORARIO DE LAURA

lunes 16	martes 17	miércoles 18	jueves 19	viernes 20	sábado 21	domingo 22
Mercedes— tenis 4:00	Sara— Café Gijón, 3:30	Mamá— regalo para Papá, 3:30	Mercedes— tenis 4:00	Roberto— Restaurante La Góndola 8:00 ♡	Mamá y Papá—	☀ → ¡PLAYA!

1. ¿Qué hacen Laura y Mercedes los lunes y los jueves?

_____

2. ¿Con quién sale Mercedes el miércoles? ¿Adónde van y qué hacen?

_____

3. ¿Con quién sale Laura el martes? ¿Qué hacen las dos chicas?

_____

4. ¿Cuándo sale Mercedes con su mamá? ¿Y cuándo sale Laura con su mamá?

_____

5. ¿Qué hace Mercedes el viernes, y con quién sale?

_____

6. ¿Qué hace Laura este fin de semana?

_____

7. ¿Cuándo sale Mercedes con su abuela? ¿Qué hacen?

_____

8. ¿Con quién sale Laura el viernes? ¿Y con quién sale Mercedes el sábado?

_____

CAPÍTULO 6 Segundo paso

■ TERCER PASO

14 Match each of the problems pictured below with the most logical solution. Can you think of another solution to each problem?

1. ____

2. ____

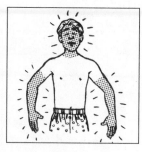

3. ____

4. ____

5. ____

6. ____

7. ____

8. ____

Soluciones

a. Debes comprar una bicicleta nueva.
b. Debes estudiar mucho antes de los exámenes finales.
c. Debes dormir *(sleep)* ahora y hacer la tarea mañana.
d. No debes ir al cine si no tienes dinero.

e. Debes caminar con el perrito por la mañana, por la tarde y por la noche.
f. No debes tomar mucho sol en la playa.
g. Debes ir al restaurante a comer algo.
h. Debes organizar tu cuarto.

15 For each party listed below, write two sentences: one stating a problem that person or group has, and another stating what the party should do or should not do. Explain your solutions to the problems as in the **modelo**.

MODELO   Nuestro colegio...
Nuestro colegio debe comprar un televisor para la cafetería porque me gusta ver televisión cuando como.

1. El profesor/La profesora de español... _____

_____

2. Mis amigos... _____

_____

3. Yo... _____

_____

4. Mis padres... _____

_____

5. Mi hermano/a... _____

_____

6. La clase de español... _____

_____

7. El director/La directora del colegio... _____

_____

16 On weekends, Irene and Merche like to get together and enjoy the free time. But sometimes it's hard to find free time, even on a Saturday morning. Follow the directions to create
a phone conversation between Irene and Merche.

Irene	Merche
Calls up Merche and asks what she is doing.	Says that she's cleaning her room now.
Asks if she wants to go to the mall this afternoon.	Says yes, but that she must do some things at home first.
Asks what she needs to do.	Mentions three chores she has to do.
Says that tomorrow she can't go out.	Asks Irene what she's going to do tomorrow.
She must wash her parents' car and visit her granddad.	Says she's sorry (**lo siento**), but she can't go out this afternoon.
Tells Merche not to worry, and ends the conversation.	Says goodbye.

CAPÍTULO 6 Tercer paso

17 It's Saturday afternoon and Roberto and his friends Javier and Silvia are throwing a party tonight at Roberto's house. They've gathered to get the house into shape for the party, and there's a lot of work to do! Look at the picture of his house below. Then write the question Robert's friends would use to ask what they should do. Next put yourself in Roberto's place and write instructions telling each person what he or she should do. Split the work up evenly and make sure Roberto does his fair share, too.

Los amigos de Roberto preguntan: _____

_____

_____

_____

18 When it comes to Calvin's duties and obligations, often Calvin and his parents have very different ideas. As you can see from the comic strip below, Calvin usually doesn't want to do what his parents want him to do.

CALVIN AND HOBBES. © Watterson. Distributed by Universal Press Syndicate. Reprinted with Permission. All Rights Reserved.

Put yourself in the place of Calvin's mom, and imagine that you are trying to get him ready for school in the morning. What do you say to him? Write three recommendations or suggestions, using (**no**) **debes** + infinitive.

_____

_____

_____

Now put yourself in Calvin's place. What do you think your mom should—or should not do? Write three things you think Calvin might say, using (**no**) **debes** + infinitive.

_____

HRW material copyrighted under notice appearing earlier in this work.

CAPÍTULO 6 Tercer paso

■ VAMOS A LEER

19 a. Below are three letters from the advice column in *Gente Joven*, a teen magazine. Read through the letters, using the reading strategies you've learned.

Querida *Gente Joven*,
Estoy desesperada y necesito su ayuda. Hay un chico en mi colegio que me gusta mucho. Se llama Francisco. Pero mis padres se oponen a° nuestra amistad°, porque piensan que es un muchacho "loco." Y ahora mis padres no me permiten hablar o salir con él. Pero quiero ser su amiga porque pienso que Francisco es una persona muy buena. ¿Qué debo hacer? **Cecilia**

se oponen a *are against, oppose*
amistad *friendship*

Querida *Gente Joven*,
Estoy preocupado por una amiga mía que se llama Elisa. Somos mejores amigos desde° el primer grado. Ahora Elisa está muy cambiada°. Ya no es la chica alegre, considerada, honesta, y trabajadora de antes. No estudia, no hace su tarea, no habla ni sale conmigo ni con sus otros amigos, siempre está cansada...su conducta no es la misma. Creo que tiene un problema muy grave, pero no sé qué hacer.
Diego

desde *since*
cambiada *changed*

Querida *Gente Joven*,
Tengo 15 años y soy una chica responsable, madura e inteligente, pero mis padres son super-estrictos conmigo. No me permiten usar el teléfono para llamar a mis amigos ni recibir llamadas°. No puedo salir durante la semana y sólo a veces los fines de semana. Mi vida es aburrida y triste. No sé por qué mis padres son así conmigo. Con mi hermano, no son tan estrictos. ¿Qué puedo hacer para ganar su confianza°? Gracias, **Amalia**

llamadas *phone calls*
confianza *confidence*

b. Answer the following questions.

1. What is the first letter about? A problem . . .

   a. at school   **b.** with parents   **c.** with a friend   **d.** at work

2. What is the second letter about? A problem . . .

   a. with money   **b.** with a brother/sister   **c.** with a friend   **d.** with parents

3. What is the third letter about? A problem . . .

   a. with a brother/sister   **b.** with a teacher   **c.** with a coach   **d.** with parents

4. In the first letter, what do the parents think of Francisco? What does Cecilia think of him?

   _____

   _____

5. In the second letter, how is Elisa normally? And how has she been lately?

   _____

   _____

6. In the third letter, how does Amalia describe herself? How does she compare her parents' treatment of her with the way her brother is treated?

   _____

   _____

c. You're a guest columnist for *Gente Joven*. Choose one letter to answer. Together, come up with at least three recommendations for solving the problem using **(no) debes** + infinitive.

   _____

   _____

CAPÍTULO 6 Vamos a leer

■ CULTURA

20 As you read in the **Nota cultural** on p. 155 of your text, god-parents are an important part of the Hispanic family. While the original function of godparents was to sponsor a child at its baptism and to take responsibility for its religious upbringing, today the **madrina** and **padrino** are also friends, advisors, and helpers to the child. They have very strong ties not only to their godchild, but also to the child's parents. The word **compadrazgo** literally means *joint paternity*. Mothers will refer to their child's godmother as **comadre** and fathers will call their child's godfather **compadre**, which also means *close friend*. Look over the greeting cards, and then work with a partner to answer the questions. Compare your answers with other classmates.

1. Can you figure out who the cards are for and what the occasion is?

   _____

   _____

2. Are cards for godparents generally found in card stores in the U.S.? Why or why not?

   _____

3. What does the fact that greeting cards exist especially for godparents tell you about their role in Spanish-speaking families?

   _____

   _____

4. Why do you think that godparents play an important part in Hispanic family life?

   _____

   _____

   _____

5. Do you have godparents? What adults are close to and important to you?

   _____

   _____

21 What kinds of generalizations can you make about privacy in the U.S. and in Spanish-speaking countries?

   _____

   _____

Nombre _____ Clase _____ Fecha _____

¿Qué te gustaría hacer?

DE ANTEMANO

1 Write the name of the **fotonovela** character next to each statement that he or she could have made. Choose from the following characters: Diego, Cristina, Pablo, or Sr. Andrade.

_____ 1. ¿Por qué Cristina no me invita a su fiesta? Somos buenos amigos...

_____ 2. ¡Pobre Diego! Está muy triste. Me gustaría ayudar...

_____ 3. ¡Qué pena! Pablo no puede ir a mi fiesta.

_____ 4. ¿Dónde debo poner este recado para Diego? Ah... aquí en la mesa está bien.

_____ 5. ¡Qué complicado! Me gustaría ir a la fiesta de Cristina, pero ya tengo planes con Diego.

2 Greg, a new exchange student in Ecuador, has a really busy week planned. Based on his calendar below, match each invitation with the correct response.

lunes	martes	miércoles	jueves	viernes	sábado	domingo
4	**5**	**6**	**7**	**8**	**9**	**10**
Reunión—Club de intercambio, 6:00 p.m.	Cita—Dr. Londoño, 4:30 p.m.	Concierto, 9:30 p.m.	Cita—Oficina del Director, 10:00 a.m.	Examen de español, 9:00 a.m.	Fiesta—Cristina Ordóñez, 8:30 p.m.	Fútbol—parque, 12:30 p.m.

_____ 1. ¿Quieres ir al cine esta noche a las seis?

_____ 2. ¿Cuándo es tu examen de español?

_____ 3. Vamos al zoológico este domingo. ¿Quieres ir también?

_____ 4. ¿Te gustaría venir a mi casa mañana después de clases?

_____ 5. Oye, vamos a ir a tomar algo ahora durante el descanso. ¿Quieres ir?

_____ 6. ¿Qué planes tienes para el sábado?

a. Es el viernes a las nueve. ¡Necesito estudiar y practicar mucho esta semana!

b. Lo siento, pero no puedo. Mañana tengo una cita con el médico a las cuatro y media de la tarde.

c. Por la noche voy a la fiesta de Cristina.

d. Creo que el domingo voy a jugar al fútbol. Pero gracias, ¿eh?

e. Gracias, pero a las seis voy a una reunión del Club de intercambio.

f. ¿Van ahora mismo? Lo siento, pero tengo que hablar con el director a las diez.

■ PRIMER PASO

3 Below are parts of two phone conversations. Use the new words and expressions on p. 183 of your textbook to complete the missing parts of the conversations.

MANUEL   ¿Aló?

ELENA   1. _____

MANUEL   ¿De parte de quién, por favor?

ELENA   2. _____

MANUEL   Elena ¿qué tal? Oye, lo siento, pero no está ahora.

ELENA   3. _____

MANUEL   Está bien.

Manuel

SRA. ALONSO   4. _____

LEONOR   Buenos días, Sra. Alonso. ¿Está Carmen, por favor?

SRA. ALONSO   5. _____

LEONOR   Soy yo, Leonor.

SRA. ALONSO   6. _____

LEONOR   Muy bien, gracias. ¿Y Ud.?

SRA. ALONSO   7. _____

LEONOR   No hay problema. Llamo más tarde.

SRA. ALONSO   8. _____

LEONOR   Bien. _____, Sra. Alonso.

SRA. ALONSO   Adiós.

Leonor

4 Sometimes Calvin answers the phone at his house and the results are not always what the callers expect. Read the following comic strip, then answer the questions.

1. What does the caller want? _____

2. Does Calvin help the caller? _____

3. Who do you think is calling in the last frame?

   _____

4. Imagine that the speech bubble in the third frame of the comic strip is empty. What could Calvin say in response to the caller's question that would be more helpful?

   _____

   _____

5 What would you invite the people shown below to do? Create an invitation for each one, based on what you think each person or group of people likes to do. Then write the other person's acceptance of the invitation.

1. TÚ _____

   _____

   TU AMIGO _____

   _____

2. TÚ _____

   _____

   TUS AMIGOS _____

   _____

3. TÚ _____

   _____

   TUS AMIGAS _____

   _____

4. TÚ _____

   _____

   TU AMIGO _____

   _____

5. TÚ _____

   _____

   TUS AMIGOS _____

   _____

6 Use the clues and the **Vocabulario** section on p. 186 of your textbook to complete the following sentences.

1. El lugar donde puedes ver animales acuáticos es el _____.

2. Un lugar donde viven muchas personas, por ejemplo Quito o Miami, es una

   _____.

3. Cuando una persona termina las clases en el colegio, a veces hay una _____

   _____ para celebrar.

4. Un lugar muy divertido, donde hay montañas rusas *(rollercoasters)*, es el

   _____.

5. La ceremonia en que un hombre y una mujer se casan *(marry)* es una_____.

6. Una fiesta para celebrar 50 años de matrimonio *(marriage)* es una _____

   _____.

7. El lugar lejos de las ciudades donde es posible ver la naturaleza *(nature)*, es el

   _____.

8. Ahora tengo 14 años. En junio, voy a cumplir 15 y voy a tener una _____

   _____.

9. El lugar donde puedes ver actores en una comedia es el _____.

10. Mis padres se casaron en 1985 y ahora van a tener una fiesta de _____.

7 Where would the people below rather go this weekend, and why? Write a sentence about each person's preferences based on the drawings.

MODELO Mario prefiere ir al circo porque quiere ver los elefantes.

1. **Esteban y Ramón**

   _____

   _____

2. **El Sr. Arco**

   _____

   _____

3. **La familia Tamayo**

   _____

   _____

4. **Nosotros**

   _____

   _____

■ SEGUNDO PASO

8 Some classmates are talking about weekend plans in the cafeteria. Read what each person has planned, then draw a line connecting the pairs of students that are going to do something together.

1. Más que nada, quiero ver los leones y los tigres, pero los elefantes son muy interesantes también.

2. Voy a pasar el sábado con mi amigo Felipe. Vamos al lago, ¡y nos vamos a divertir muchísimo!

3. Mi grupo favorito "Sabor tropical" va a tocar este sábado. ¡Son increíbles!

4. Antonio tiene dos entradas *(tickets)* para el nuevo parque de atracciones. Me encantan los parques de atracciones. ¡Pienso subir a la montaña rusa *(rollercoaster)* 50 veces!

a. Hay tantas cosas que hacer allí. Pienso nadar y tomar el sol.

b. Me gustaría mucho salir con Marisol este fin de semana. Ella quiere ir al parque de atracciones, pero a mí la montaña rusa no me gusta.

c. Mi prima Juanita y yo pensamos ir al zoológico el domingo. A ella le fascinan los animales.

d. Creo que Amalia y yo vamos a salir. Pensamos asistir a un concierto de música caribeña en el Teatro Central.

9 Araceli and Manolo are planning what they're going to do this weekend. Complete their conversation with the correct forms of the following verbs.

gustaría	pensar
querer ir	preferir

MANOLO   Oye, Araceli, ¿qué _____ hacer este fin de semana?

ARACELI   Pues, no sé. ¿Qué _____ a hacer tú?

MANOLO   Bueno, (yo) _____ ir al lago, pero mis hermanitos

_____ jugar al tenis conmigo. Pero no me gusta mucho jugar al

tenis; _____ nadar. ¿Te _____ ir al lago conmigo?

ARACELI   Sí, me _____... pero, ¿cuándo _____ ir?

_____ ir el sábado porque el domingo por la tarde

_____ al museo con Guillermo.

10 Emilio is talking to Alejandra about weekend plans. Using the expressions **ir** + **a** + infinitive and **pensar** + infinitive, write what Emilio would say about his plans, how he would ask about Alejandra's plans, and what she would say Víctor and the other two boys are planning to do.

MODELO

Amador

Amador va a ir al parque este fin de semana. Piensa jugar al fútbol con sus amigos.

1.

Emilio

_____

_____

_____

2.

Alejandra

¿Y tú, Alejandra? ¿ _____ ?

¿ _____

_____ ?

3.

Víctor

_____

_____

4.

Rafa y José Luis

_____

_____

_____

¡Ven conmigo! Level 1, Chapter 7

11 This Saturday Gustavo has a lot of plans. Write at least five sentences describing his day, using the illustrations as a guide and the expressions in the box below.

> ir + a + ...
>
> pensar + ...
>
> necesitar + ...
>
> querer + ...
>
> A Gustavo le gustaría + ...

_____

_____

_____

_____

_____

_____

12 The Montemayors are going out with some friends tonight. Complete the following sentences with what each person needs to do to get ready according to the cues. Start with Mrs. Montemayor asking her husband if everyone is ready.

1. ¿ _____?

2.  No, mi amor. Marco _____

3.  Y yo _____

4. Creo que tú _____

5.  Luego Marisa _____

6.  Y por último, Pepe _____

■ TERCER PASO

13 The strip below shows a conversation between Calvin and his friend Susi. Read the cartoon, then answer the questions.

¡HOBBES! ¡HOBBES! ¿DÓNDE ESTÁS?

HOLA, CALVIN. ¿NO QUIERES VENIR A TOMAR EL TE?

NADA, NADA. ESTOY BUSCANDO A MI MEJOR AMIGO, SECUESTRADO POR UN PERRO. DÉJAME EN PAZ.

PUES EL SEÑOR CALVIN ES UN GROSERO. ¿NO CREE USTED? ¿ALGUIEN QUIERE MÁS TE?

CALVIN AND HOBBES. © Watterson. Distributed by Universal Press Syndicate. Reprinted with Permission. All Rights Reserved.

1. Hobbes is Calvin's toy tiger. Where is Hobbes in the strip above?

   _____

2. What phrase does Susi use in the second scene to extend an invitation to Calvin ?

   _____

3. What's his answer and why do you think he answers this way?

   _____

4. What does Susi think of Calvin because of the way he answered?

   _____

14 How else could Calvin have responded to Susi's invitation? Imagine that you are the cartoonist, and create three new responses for Calvin.

   a. an acceptance

   _____

   _____

   b. a refusal with an excuse

   _____

   _____

   c. a suggestion that he and Susi do something else

   _____

   _____

15 Luisa and Marcos were passing notes to each other in study hall. Match up what Marcos wrote on the left with Luisa's sentences on the right. Number Luisa's sentences in the correct order to find out what they were discussing. When you finish, read through the note in order and answer the questions below.

Marcos　　　　　　　　　　　　　　**Luisa**

1. ¿Qué vas a hacer este sábado?　　　—　　Bueno, ¿te gustaría estudiar conmigo? A mí me gusta el álgebra.

3. Porque tengo que hacer la tarea de álgebra y es muy difícil.　　—　　Buena idea... siempre tengo ganas de comer algo después de estudiar.

5. ¿En serio? Gracias... me gustaría mucho. ¿A qué hora quieres estudiar?　　—　　Por la mañana, nada, pero por la tarde, voy a salir. ¿Por qué?

7. ¡Perfecto! Y después, si quieres, vamos a comer una hamburguesa.　　—　　No sé... ¿Por qué no vienes a mi casa a las diez? Así podemos estudiar juntos.

16 Based of the information in Activity 15 indicate whether each statement is true or false. Correct the false ones.

1. Luisa no tiene planes para el sábado.

_____

2. Marcos tiene que estudiar para un examen de historia.

_____

3. Marcos y Luisa piensan estudiar juntos el sábado por la mañana.

_____

4. Después de estudiar con Luisa, Marcos tiene prisa para ir al trabajo.

_____

5. Luisa siempre tiene sueño después de estudiar.

_____

17 Joaquín has just called some friends to come over and watch videos this afternoon. Based on what you see in the pictures, how do his friends respond? Include Joaquín's invitation and his friends' excuses in each conversation. Use the following expressions: **tener que** + infinitive, **tener sueño**, **(no) tener ganas de** + infinitive, and **tener prisa**.

Jimena

Juanito

Fernanda

Roberto

JOAQUÍN _____

_____

JIMENA _____

_____

JOAQUÍN _____

_____

JUANITO _____

_____

JOAQUÍN _____

_____

FERNANDA _____

_____

JOAQUÍN _____

_____

ROBERTO _____

_____

18 Anita has been invited to a graduation party, and she's really looking forward to it. Imagine that she's thinking aloud about the party. Write a short paragraph including: what she plans to do at the party, what she does and doesn't feel like doing at the party, and what she has to do to get ready for the party. Use the following verb expressions.

Tengo que		Voy a	Me gustaría		Necesito	
	Quiero			Pienso		Tengo ganas de

_____

_____

_____

_____

¡Ven conmigo! Level 1, Chapter 7

▓ VAMOS A LEER

19 In the U.S., we tend to take having a phone for granted. However, in some parts of Spain and Latin America, having a telephone in one's home can be the exception rather than the rule. Residents may be put on a long waiting list to have a phone line installed and to get a telephone. Also both local and long-distance calls are extremely expensive. For these reasons, it is not unusual for people in Spanish-speaking countries to use public phone booths or **Telefónicas** (*calling centers*) instead of having a phone at home.

Knowing a little about phones in Spanish-speaking countries can help you understand the reading. Here is a page from a phone book. Look it over, then answer the questions below.

1. El teléfono es una parte importante de la vida. Aprécielo en todo su valor.

2. El bloque de conexión de su teléfono es delicado. Hay que protegerlo.

3. El teléfono no es un juguete. Controle su uso.

4. Sus hijos no deben hacer su tarea por teléfono. Use el teléfono en forma mesurada.

5. No debe monopolizar el teléfono de la oficina. Sea breve.

6. El teléfono es un instrumento delicado. Cuídelo bien.

1. What is this information about?
   a. how to get directory assistance
   b. how to use phones properly

2. Look at number 3. Based on the drawing, what do you think this rule is saying?
   a. phones are not toys
   b. babies can play with the phone as long as no one needs to use it

3. What do numbers 1, 2, and 6 all have in common?
   a. they say that the telephone is part of modern life
   b. they urge taking care of the phone and the phone connections

4. Numbers 4 and 5 are also similar. What do they all recommend doing?
   a. keeping phone conversations at home and work brief
   b. talking on the phone for a long time at night when the rates are lowest

■ CULTURA

20 As you read in the **Nota cultural** on p. 189 of your textbook, public transportation is a bigger part of day-to-day life in Spanish-speaking countries than in the U.S. It's not uncommon in larger cities, such as Buenos Aires, Madrid, or Mexico City, for people not to own a car, but to rely instead on the subway or bus systems for transportation. In Spain, the subway is called **el metro**, while in Buenos Aires, it's referred to as **el subte** (short for **el subterráneo**). A public bus in Uruguay and Argentina is **un colectivo** or **un ómnibus**, **una guagua** in Puerto Rico and Cuba, and **un autobús** in Spain. Answer the questions below.

1. How do you generally get to school, to work, and to after-school activities? How do you get around on the weekends?

   _____

   _____

2. Do you have a driver's license and access to a car?

   _____

   _____

3. Is there a bus or subway system where you live? Do you ever use it? Why or why not?

   _____

   _____

4. What are the advantages and disadvantages of using a car as your main means of transportation?

   _____

   _____

5. What are the advantages and disadvantages of getting around using a public transportation system?

   _____

   _____

6. Can you imagine living in your area without a car? What would you do instead?

   _____

   _____

21 Now imagine that you're a student living in Buenos Aires, the capital city of Argentina and you don't have a car. Describe how you get around. What are some advantages and disadvantages?

_____

_____

_____

_____

CAPÍTULO

8

¡A comer!

■ DE ANTEMANO

1 Who orders what in the **fotonovela**? Look over the story on pp. 204–205 of your textbook, then match each character with what he or she orders.

Diego

empanadas

plátanos

agua

sancocho

carne colorada

legumbres

Cristina

Chen

Raúl

2 Match the different characters' questions on the left with answers on the right. Write the letter of the best response to each question in the blank.

_____ 1. Raúl, ¿qué es carne colorada?

_____ 2. Cristina, ¿por qué no vas a pedir el sancocho?

_____ 3. Diego, ¿no quieres otra empanada?

_____ 4. Bueno, Chen... ¿qué tal está el sancocho?

_____ 5. Tengo sed todavía. ¿Vamos a pedir otra botella de agua?

a. Está riquísimo. ¿Quieres un poco?

b. ¡Cuidado! La sopa está muy caliente.

c. ¿Por qué no pides dos? El ají aquí está super-picante.

d. Porque comemos sancocho en casa casi todas las semanas. Hoy quiero empanadas.

e. Es un plato de carne, muy típico del Ecuador... a mí me encanta.

f. No, gracias. Están muy buenas, pero no puedo comer más.

Nombre _____ Clase _____ Fecha _____

■ PRIMER PASO

3 Breakfast at the Montalvo house is often complicated because each person likes to have something different. Using each drawing, write a sentence asking Luis what each member of the family has for breakfast and then write Luis's answers.

 1.
Raquel y Esteban

 2.
Luis

 3.
Sr. Montalvo

 4.
Sra. Montalvo

1. _____

2. _____

3. _____

4. _____

4 Breakfast is the most important meal of the day, but not everyone eats a good breakfast. What nutritional advice do you have for the following people? Based on each person's comments, write one or two sentences telling each one what he or she should eat for breakfast.

MODELO   Nunca tomo desayuno. Por las mañanas siempre tengo prisa.
Si siempre tienes prisa, debes comer uno o dos plátanos, pan tostado y un vaso de leche.

1. DIANA   Estoy a dieta, y por eso no desayuno nunca.

    TÚ _____

2. CHEMA   ¡Uf! No me gusta comer por las mañanas.

    TÚ _____

3. EUGENIA Me gustan mucho los huevos y el tocino... pero tienen mucho colesterol.

    TÚ _____

4. DIEGO   Soy alérgico a *(allergic to)* la leche y el yogurt.

    TÚ _____

5. CHUY   El médico dice que necesito comer más fruta fresca.

    TÚ _____

6. MARÍA   ¡Siempre lo mismo! Cereal con leche. Quiero comer algo más interesante de vez en cuando.

    TÚ _____

86 Practice and Activity Book

¡Ven conmigo! Level 1, Chapter 8

HRW material copyrighted under notice appearing earlier in this work.

5 How do you feel about the following foods? Explain how often you eat them, using **encantar** and **gustar**. Then tell why you like or don't like each one. Is there a food that you really don't like at all? Write about it in number 7.

1.  _____
_____

4. 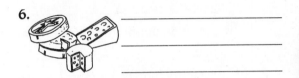 _____
_____

2. _____
_____

5. 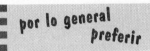 _____
_____

3. _____
_____

6. _____
_____

7. _____
_____

6 It's late morning and everyone's hungry and thinking about his or her favorite lunch. Write what each of the people in the picture love to have for lunch, using one of the expressions from the box.

por lo general
preferir

Victoria   Héctor   Lupe   Sebastián

1. _____
_____

2. _____
_____

3. _____
_____

4. _____
_____

Nombre _____ Clase _____ Fecha _____

7 A Spanish-speaking magazine is doing a survey to find out more about the eating habits of high-school students. Take part in the survey by completing the questionnaire below.

Cuestionario, 1ª parte

1. Cuando estoy enfermo(a), me encanta(n)... _____
_____

2. Por lo general, no me gusta(n) para nada... _____
_____

3. Para el desayuno, me encanta tomar... _____
_____

4. Después del almuerzo, me encanta comer... _____
_____

5. Antes de dormir me encanta comer... _____
_____

6. Cuando salgo con mis amigos, nos encanta comer... _____
_____

7. Los domingos por la mañana me encanta tomar... _____
_____

8. Por lo general, almuerzo a las... _____
_____

8 Luisa is babysitting and Sra. Benavides has left a note explaining what each of the Benavides children can and can't eat. Complete her note with forms of the verb **poder** and other words and phrases as needed.

Querida Luisa,

Para el almuerzo, Miguelito 1. _____ comer un sándwich de crema de maní. No 2. _____ comer muchas papitas. Susanita y Carlitos 3. _____ comer la sopa de verduras. Y tú 4. _____ comer la sopa o comer un sándwich también. De postre todos 5. _____ comer fruta.

Para la cena, Susanita no 6. _____ comer el pollo porque tiene alergias. Ella 7. _____ comer una hamburguesa. Carlitos y Miguelito 8. _____ comer el pollo o los espaguetis. De postre, tú 9. _____ comer helado, si quieres... ¡pero los niños no 10. _____ comer mucho helado!

Si tienes un problema, 11. _____ hablar con la vecina, Sra. Aguirre. ¿Y tú, Luisa? ¿Qué 12. _____ por lo 13. _____ para el desayuno? ¿Y qué quieres 14. _____ tu almuerzo?

Buena suerte con todo, y gracias.

Sra. Benavides

▓ SEGUNDO PASO

9 Everyone has a particular food that he or she can't stand. Read the following cartoon to find out what it is that Juanito hates.

¡Guácala! ¡Qué asco!   *Yuck! Gross!*
¿Ya terminaste los coles de Bruselas?   *Have you finished your Brussels sprouts?*

How would Juanito answer the question **¿Cómo están los coles de Bruselas?** Circle the number of each sentence below that matches Juanito's reaction to his dinner.

1. "Están deliciosos."

2. "No me gustan para nada estos coles de Bruselas ."

3. "¡Estos coles de Bruselas están fríos y salados!"

4. "¡Uf! No puedo comer estos coles de Bruselas."

5. "Los coles de Bruselas de mi mamá siempre están muy ricos."

6. "Me encanta comer en esta casa."

10 What would you ask or say in the following situations? Using phrases from p. 212 of your textbook and other phrases you know, write two or three sentences to respond to each situation. Be honest, but remember to be polite!

1. You and your friend have swapped lunches today. When you bite into his sandwich, you realize that it's liverwurst and onion.

_____

_____

2. For your mom's birthday, you've made her favorite meal. You want to know what she thinks of the main course and dessert.

_____

_____

3. As a surprise, your friend invites you to dinner and serves a recipe she just made up on her own: spinach-sardine casserole.

_____

_____

4. The waiter at your favorite restaurant asks how your meal is.

_____

_____

5. When you come home from school, someone's been baking and the kitchen is full of chocolate chip cookies.

_____

_____

11 Look at the **Nota gramatical** on p. 212 of your textbook. Remember that **ser** is used to describe general or typical characteristics of a food. **Estar** is used to describe how particular dishes taste, seem, or look. For each English sentence below, choose the form of **ser** or **estar** to complete the Spanish equivalent.

MODELO   These cookies taste great.
     Estas galletas (son/están) muy ricas.
     Here **están** is the right answer, because the sentence is talking about how these cookies taste, not what cookies in general are like.

1. Soup is good when you're sick.
 La sopa (es /está) buena cuando estás enfermo/a.

2. Careful! This pizza is really hot!
 ¡Cuidado! Esta pizza (es /está) muy caliente.

3. Yuck! The spaghetti is cold.
 ¡Qué asco! Los espaguetis (son /están) fríos.

4. Mexican food is spicy, right?
 La comida mexicana (es /está) picante, ¿verdad?

5. I love chocolate ice cream. It's delicious.
 Me encanta el helado de chocolate. (Es /Está) muy rico.

6. Hmm . . . this jelly doesn't taste very sweet.
 Mmm... esta jalea no (es /está) muy dulce.

7. Milk is good for children.
 La leche (es /está) buena para los niños.

12 In this chapter you've learned how to say more things with the verb **tener**. Do you remember other expressions with **tener** as well? Describe each of the following pictures using at least three expressions with **tener**.

_____

_____

_____

_____

_____

_____

1. Arturo

HRW material copyrighted under notice appearing earlier in this work.

CAPÍTULO 8 Segundo paso

_____
_____
_____
_____
_____
_____
_____
_____
_____

2. **Celia**

13 You want to take a survey on eating habits of high school students. Complete this set of questions by asking what students eat or drink

  1) when they're hungry or thirsty after class

  2) when they're in a hurry

  3) when they need a quick lunch

Cuestionario, *2a parte*

1. Cuando tengo mucha sed después de clase, me gusta tomar... _____
_____

2. Cuando tengo mucha _____
_____

3. Por lo general, _____

4. Mi almuerzo favorito _____
_____

5. Por la noche, siempre tengo ganas de comer... _____
_____

6. Si no tengo sueño, por lo general puedo dormir después de comer... _____
_____

7. Si no tengo mucha hambre para el desayuno, como... _____
_____

■ TERCER PASO

14 Find out what seven items you need to set the table by placing the syllables in the correct order. Then write the words out below.

| cu | so | vi | ta | pla | lle | ne | cha | zón | cu | to | ta | llo | te | chi | ra | ser | dor | va |

Necesito una _____, un _____, un _____, una

_____, un _____, un _____ y un _____.

15 Look over the vocabulary for this chapter to complete the crossword puzzle below.

Horizontales
2. La primera comida del día.
6. Una comida que se come *(is eaten)* con jalea en un sándwich.
9. Un marisco *(seafood)* pequeño.
10. Una bebida con mucha vitamina C.
11. Una bebida fría que se hace con limones.
12. Un tipo de legumbre anaranjada.
13. La lista de comidas en un restaurante se llama el ___.
14. La cosa que se usa *(is used)* para limpiar la boca *(mouth)* después de comer.
15. Una legumbre verde y un ingrediente importante en una ensalada.

Verticales
1. Antes de pagar en un restaurante, necesitas pedir la ___.
3. La comida después del desayuno.
4. Una fruta cítrica, más grande que *(bigger than)* una naranja.
5. La comida después del almuerzo.
7. Una agua especial que se sirve *(is served)* en botellas.
8. El atún y el salmón son tipos de ___.
9. La hamburguesa se hace *(is made)* con ___.

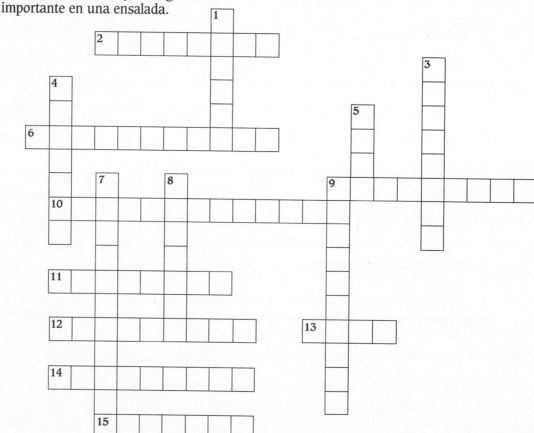

¡Ven conmigo! Level 1, Chapter 8

16 You're at the **Café El Rincón** for dinner with a large group of friends. It's your waiter's first day on the job, and he keeps making mistakes with everyone's order. All of the things pictured below are things that he needs to bring you. How would you politely ask for them?

1. tres

   _____
   _____

2. otro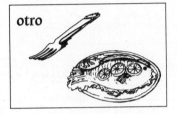

   _____
   _____

3.

   _____
   _____

4. un   limpio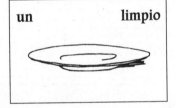

   _____
   _____

5. otra

   _____
   _____

6. otra

   _____
   _____

17 Manuel, Marimar and Sofía are eating out to celebrate Marimar's birthday. Fill in the dialogue according to what takes place in the illustration.

Manuel   Marimar   Sofía   Camarera

SOFÍA   Bueno, Marimar, ¿qué _____?

MARIMAR   _____ a pedir_____

SOFÍA   Debes pedir una ensalada también. Ah, aquí viene la camarera.

CAMARERA   _____

SOFÍA   ¿Para mí? Bueno, yo _____

MARIMAR   A mí _____. Ah, y _____, también.

CAMARERA   Muy bien. Y a usted señor, ¿qué le _____ traer?

MANUEL   _____

CAMARERA   Muy bien. ¿Y qué les _____ de tomar?

SOFÍA   _____

CAMARERA   ¿Desean algo más? ¿Algún postre?

SOFÍA   _____

18 You and your friends just finished the meal detailed on this restaurant bill. Create a brief conversation in which the server asks if you want anything else, you answer no and ask for the bill, he or she tells you how much the meal is, and you find out if the tip is included.

_____

_____

_____

_____

_____

_____

_____

El Ranchero

Calle Blanca 44
28012 Madrid   Nº 004169

Cantidad	CONCEPTO	Pesetas
1	Mixta	360
1	Judias verdes	450
1	Salmon	1100
1	Tortilla	300
2	Pan	200
1	Agua	150
1	Vino	150
1	Bombon glace	300
1	Cafe	100
	TOTAL	

■ VAMOS A LEER

19 As you read in the **Nota cultural** on p. 210 of your textbook, lunch (**la comida**) is the main meal of the day in Spanish-speaking countries. It usually consists of a lighter **primer plato** *(first course)* of soup, pasta, vegetables, etc., and is followed by a more substantial **segundo plato** *(main course)* of meat, chicken, or fish. Dessert, often consisting of fresh fruit, is also part of the meal. If this type of lunch seems like a lot of food to you, remember that most Spanish speakers have lighter breakfasts and dinners than we do in the U.S.

Below is a restaurant menu from Spain. As part of the **menú del día** *(daily specials)*, diners choose one **primer plato** and one **segundo plato**, plus **postre** *(dessert)*, in any combination, for a fixed price. Look over the menu, then answer the questions below.

> Menú del día   1100 pesetas
> Pan, agua o vino y postre incluidos
>
> 1er plato
> Espaguetis
> Ensalada mixta
> Sopa de fideos°   *noodles*
> Tortilla° de jamón   *omelet*
>
> 2ndo plato
> Filete de bistec
> Bonito° con tomate   *tuna*
> Pollo asado°   *roasted*
> Gambas al ajillo°   *shrimp in garlic sauce*
>
> Postre
> Arroz con leche°   *rice pudding*
> Fruta del tiempo
> Helados variados

1. Which dishes from the **1er plato** group have pasta? Do any dishes have meat? If so, which ones?

   _____

   _____

2. What are the seafood dishes in the **2ndo plato** group? If you didn't like seafood, what could you have instead as your second course?

   _____

   _____

3. What would be a good **1er plato** to eat if it's cold outside? What about if you're on a diet?

   _____

   _____

4. Look at the choices under **Postre**. What do you think the words **del tiempo** mean when referring to fruit? What does **helados variados** tell you about the assortment of flavors of ice cream this restaurant has?

   _____

   _____

CAPÍTULO 8 Vamos a leer

■ CULTURA

20 While cereal is the most popular breakfast food in the U.S., it's not as common in Spanish-speaking countries. As you read in the **Nota cultural** on p. 209 of your textbook, breakfast in most Spanish-speaking countries is pretty light. Besides the foods mentioned in your textbook, people will often have **galletas** (crispy, not-too-sweet cookies, sort of like graham crackers) or **magdalenas** (small sweet rolls that taste like pound cake) with breakfast, dunking them in their coffee, chocolate, or milk. If this seems like a skimpy breakfast to you, remember that it's common for people to have a mid-morning **merienda**, or snack, at about 10:00 or 11:00 to tide them over until lunch.

a. Compare breakfast in your house and what you know about breakfast in Spanish-speaking countries. Which style of breakfast do you like better, and why?

_____

_____

b. Which seems healthier to you? What are the advantages and disadvantages of each?

_____

_____

21 Look at the **Nota cultural** on p. 214 of your textbook. You may have been surprised to learn that Ecuadorean food is not spicy. In the U.S., a common belief is that food in all Spanish-speaking countries is similar to the spicy dishes of Mexico. Such beliefs about food go both ways. For example, many people in other countries believe that everyone in the U.S. eats fast food all the time.

a. In your opinion, is **la comida norteamericana** really just fast food, or is it something else? Explain.

_____

_____

b. Now make a list of five or six breakfast, lunch, dinner, or dessert dishes that you would recommend to a Spanish-speaking tourist who wants to try some "American food."

_____

_____

22 How would you like to go home at midday, eat with your family, and take a short nap or watch TV before going back to classes? While the idea might seem strange to you, it's part of the everyday routine for many students in Spanish-speaking countries, and to them, what you do and eat at lunchtime might seem unusual. Briefly describe your lunchtime routine and compare it to the routine described above. If you could choose, which routine would you rather have?

_____

_____

_____

_____

¡Vamos de compras!

■ DE ANTEMANO

1 As the three friends from the **fotonovela** go shopping, they ask each other a lot of questions. **Can you match up each question with the most logical answer below?**

_____ 1. ¿Qué le gusta a Héctor?

_____ 2. Héctor practica muchos deportes, ¿verdad?

_____ 3. ¿Qué te parece esta blusa?

_____ 4. Oye, ¿cuánto cuestan esos bluejeans?

_____ 5. Podemos comprarle un libro, ¿no?

a. Me parece muy elegante... pero es un poco cara, ¿no?

b. Sí, tal vez podemos regalarle unos zapatos de tenis.

c. Ya tiene muchísimos libros. Prefiero regalarle algo más original.

d. ¡Buena idea! La zapatería está aquí al lado.

e. Le gusta prácticamente todo... escuchar música, ir al cine, bailar, salir...

f. Cuestan $40.00. ¡Qué caro!

2 Decide whether each of the following statements is **cierto (c)** or **falso (f)** according to the **fotonovela**.

_____ 1. Héctor quiere comprarles un regalo a las tres chicas para su graduación.

_____ 2. Eva, Lisa y Gabi entran en la tienda de ropa nada más para mirar.

_____ 3. Las tres chicas compran muchas cosas en la tienda de ropa.

_____ 4. A Gabi le gusta la falda de algodón. Dice que es una ganga.

_____ 5. Gabi piensa comprarle un libro a Héctor.

_____ 6. Cada una de las tres chicas le compra el mismo regalo a Héctor.

▇ PRIMER PASO

3 Emily is asking Esteban what gifts he plans to give different members of his family. First write Emily's questions, using the picture cues below and expressions from **Así se dice** on page 237 of your textbook. Then go back and write Esteban's answers to each question.

| Abuelo | Abuela | Papá | Mamá | Luisito | Maripili |

Emily wants to know...

1. whom the wallet is for _____

_____

2. what Esteban plans to buy for his sister _____

_____

3. what type of gift he is looking for for grandfather _____

_____

4. whom the earrings are for _____

_____

5. what Esteban plans to give his mom _____

_____

6. whom the compact disc is for _____

_____

4 Read the descriptions of some of María's friends. Based on what you find out, what gift do you think María is going to give to each of them? Follow the model.

MODELO   A Amalia le encantan las películas viejas.
          María le va a regalar un video de una película de John Wayne.

1. A su amigo Tomás le gusta la ropa formal.

_____

2. A su amiga Margarita le encantan las joyas (*jewelry*).

_____

3. A Juan Pedro y a Mario les encanta la música. Escuchan música todo el tiempo.

_____

4. Su amiga Olga está enferma.

_____

5. A Antonio le gusta mucho trabajar en el jardín.

_____

6. Sus primos Miguelito y Javier sólo tienen seis y cinco años.

_____

5 Fill in the word puzzle with the words defined below. If you complete the puzzle correctly, in the vertical column you will find the answer to the question **¿Qué buscas en el centro comercial?**

1. El tipo de tienda donde se venden caramelos.
2. En esta tienda grande, hay de todo: ropa, televisores, camas, escritorios... ¡todo!
3. Para comprar comida, puedes ir a una tienda de ___.
4. En esta tienda se vende comida, y también se venden cosméticos, detergentes, plantas y otras cosas.
5. El tipo de tienda donde se venden galletas y pan dulce.
6. Para comprar pan, debes ir a una ___.
7. Para comprar una novela o una revista, necesitas ir a una ___.
8. Si te gustan los diamantes y las perlas, tu tienda favorita es la ___.
9. La tienda favorita de los niños pequeños.
10. Si necesitas unos zapatos de tenis, vas a la ___.
11. Para comprar cuadernos y lápices, puedes ir a una ___.
12. En esta tienda, se venden rosas, tulipanes, plantas y muchas cosas más.

1. _ ▢ _ _ _ _ _ _
2. _ _ _ _ _ ▢
3. _ _ _ _ _ _ ▢ _ _
4. _ ▢ _ _ _ _ _ _
5. _ _ _ ▢ _ _
6. _ _ _ ▢ _ _
7. _ _ ▢ _ _ _
8. _ _ _ ▢ _ _
9. _ _ ▢ _ _ _
10. _ _ _ ▢ _ _ _
11. _ _ _ ▢ _ _ _
12. _ _ ▢ _ _ _

6 Adrián is new in town and is still figuring out where everything is. Imagine that you've lived there a long time and know your way around. Use the picture to write five different questions Adrián might ask you about where things are. Use **¿verdad?** and **¿no?** to form the questions.

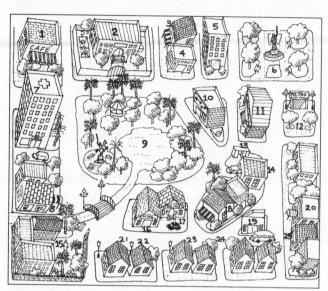

1. Café
2. Colegio
3. Florería
4. Correos
5. Almacén
6. Plaza de Armas
7. Hospital
8. Cine Bolívar
9. Parque Central
10. Gimnasio
11. Teatro Colón
12. Metro
13. Teléfonos
14. Garaje
15. Hotel San Martín
16. Zapatería
17. Policía
18. Pastelería
19. Juguetería
20. Tienda de comestibles
21. Casa de Julia
22. Casa de Adrián
23. Casa de Rafael
24. Casa de Enriqueta
25. Panadería

MODELO   la pastelería/la policía
La pastelería está al lado de la policía, ¿verdad?

1. el gimnasio/el Teatro Colón

_____

2. el almacén/el café

_____

3. la florería/el colegio

_____

4. el parque central/el hospital

_____

5. la juguetería/el Hotel San Martín

_____

¡Ven conmigo! Level 1, Chapter 9

■ SEGUNDO PASO

7 **¡Qué desastre!** Your suitcase got lost on your flight from San Antonio to Cozumel, México, and now you have to fill out a lost baggage claim form. First fill out the top part of the form, then think of at least six articles of clothing you'd be likely to take on a week-long trip to Cozumel (a beach resort with plenty of archaelogical wonders nearby) and list them in the section of the form marked **Descripción del contenido**. Be sure to specify color and fabric, using the vocabulary on pp. 242 and 243 of your textbook.

Hoja de reclamación—Irregularidad de equipaje			
Nombre y apellido(s) del pasajero	Answers will vary.		
Dirección permanente y teléfono			
No. de vuelo 887	Mes marzo	Día 14	De/A San Antonio/Cozumel
Descripción del contenido			

8 Rufino is a new exchange student from Spain. In Spain, he often dresses up. He wants to know how he should dress in order to fit in with American students. Help him out by offering advice about what to wear in the following situations to be both comfortable and in style.

MODELO   para ir a una fiesta
Para ir a una fiesta no tienes que llevar ropa muy formal. Puedes llevar unos bluejeans y una camisa de algodón.

1. para cenar en un restaurante elegante

_____

_____

2. para hacer un picnic con unos amigos

_____

_____

3. para ir a clases en el invierno

_____

_____

CAPÍTULO 9 Segundo paso

4. para salir con una chica

_____

_____

5. para ir de compras

_____

_____

6. para ir a la pizzería con unos amigos

_____

_____

7. para ir a un partido de fútbol del colegio en el otoño

_____

_____

9 Can you come up with things that fit the following descriptions? You may use vocabulary from this chapter and earlier chapters. For additional vocabulary, see pp. 242–246 of your textbook.

MODELO   algo más pequeño que una calculadora
Unos aretes son más pequeños que una calculadora.

1. algo más feo que una cucaracha *(cockroach)*

_____

2. algo más grande que un elefante

_____

3. algo más delgado que una serpiente

_____

4. alguien más famoso que el presidente

_____

5. algo más difícil que un examen de español

_____

6. algo más caro que un coche nuevo

_____

7. algo más barato que un disco compacto

_____

8. algo menos de moda que los pantalones de cuadros

_____

_____

10 Christine is visiting San Antonio. Today she's shopping at **El Mercado** for gifts from Mexico to give her family. First, complete Christine's questions by filling in the materials and patterns things are made of. Then, using the picture, help Christine decide what to buy by making comparisons between the things she mentions. In giving her your advice, consider price as well as what you think of each item.

1. ¿Qué le compro a mi papá? ¿Un cinturón, una cartera de _____ o una camisa?

_____

_____

2. Y para mi mamá, ¿cuál es mejor—el vestido o la bolsa?

_____

_____

3. ¿Qué le debo comprar a mi hermano Keith? ¿Un sombrero mexicano o un suéter de _____?

_____

_____

4. ¿Y a mi hermana Kelly? ¿Le compro el vestido de _____ o la blusa de _____?

_____

_____

5. ¿Qué le compro a mi hermano Doug? ¿Las sandalias o la chaqueta de _____ ?

_____

_____

■ TERCER PASO

11 María and her friend Clara don't agree on much of anything. Read what María has to say about the following clothing items and then choose what you think her friend Clara would say.

_____ 1. Esta falda es muy bonita. ¿no?

_____ 2. Me encantan estos zapatos. ¿Te gustan?

_____ 3. Esta chaqueta está de moda, ¿no crees?

_____ 4. $50 dólares por un cinturón. ¡Qué barato!

_____ 5. Las botas negras son feas, ¿verdad?

_____ 6. Este traje de baño no me queda muy bien.

_____ 7. Ese suéter azul es de lana.

_____ 8. Me gusta la falda de cuadros. ¿Cuál prefieres, la de rayas o la de cuadros?

_____ 9. Los pantalones son muy largos.

a. No, son bonitas.

b. ¡Qué va! *(No way!)* ¡Es un robo!

c. No. Es que te ves muy bien.

d. Bueno, yo prefiero esos negros.

e. No, es fea.

f. No. Creo que es de algodón.

g. Pues, en realidad son bastante cortos.

h. La de rayas. Además, la otra no te queda bien.

i. Bueno, en realidad ya pasó *(it's out)* de moda. Además, es fea.

12 Imagine that you're out shopping with a few friends at a thrift store. Each of them wants your advice about the clothes he or she is looking at. Answer their questions honestly!

1.

Oye, ¿cuál de estas camisas prefieres? A mí me gusta la amarilla, y además, mira, ¡me queda perfectamente!

_____

_____

2.

¿Qué traje de baño te gusta más? ¿El morado o el anaranjado? Es que me gustan los dos.

_____

_____

3.

¿Cuáles de estos pantalones te gustan más? ¿Los verdes o los de cuadros?

_____

_____

4.

¿Qué chaqueta te gusta más? ¿Esta chaqueta gris o esa chaqueta parda?

_____

_____

13 Below are some conversations between shoppers and store owners in El Mercado. Complete each conversation with demonstrative adjectives from the box.

esas   esa   esos   este
estos   esta   ese   estas

— Perdón, señor. ¿Cuánto cuesta **1.** _____ *(this)* vestido? ¿Y qué precio tienen

2. _____ *(those)* pendientes?

— **3.** _____ *(That)* vestido cuesta $40.00. Y **4.** _____ *(those)* pendientes cuestan $28.00.

_____

— Arturo, ¿ves **5.** _____ *(those)* camisetas allí? Me gustan mucho.

— ¿De veras? Prefiero **6.** _____ *(these)* camisetas aquí.

_____

— **7.** _____ *(These)* sandalias son menos caras que las otras de la otra tienda.

— Sí, pero **8.** _____ *(those)* sandalias de la otra tienda son más bonitas.

_____

— Perdón, señorita... ¿Es **9.** _____ *(this)* cinturón de cuero?

— Sí, joven. Todos **10.** _____ *(those)* cinturones allí son de cuero de muy buena calidad.

— ¿Y **11.** _____ *(these)* carteras también?

— Sí, sí. Todo lo que vendemos aquí es de cuero... zapatos, sandalias, cinturones...

14 The Estrada family is having a garage sale. Imagine you're at the sale, pointing things out to a friend. Look over the list of some of the things for sale. First tell your friend how much each thing costs and then comment on the price using the vocabulary on p. 248 of your textbook.

MODELO   una blusa de seda por $4.00
             Esta blusa de seda cuesta $4.00. ¡Qué ganga!

1. un estéreo viejo por $75.00

   _____

   _____

2. una bicicleta para un niño por $12.00

   _____

   _____

3. 3 suéteres de lana por $10.00

   _____

   _____

CAPÍTULO 9 Tercer paso

4. unos juegos de mesa por $2.00 cada uno

_____

_____

5. 4 corbatas feas por $15.00

_____

_____

6. unos vestidos de señora de algodón por $30.00 cada uno

_____

_____

15 Imagine that you and a friend are shopping in a clothing store. You're looking for a new pair of pants and your friend is looking for a new shirt. You've narrowed it down to two pairs of pants, one white ($30) and one blue ($38), while your friend must choose between one brown shirt ($26) and one shirt with green stripes ($24). Using what you've learned in this **paso**, write a dialogue between you and your friend as you ask for and give each other advice on how your respective clothing choices look and how much they cost. Each of you should have at least four lines of dialogue.

_____

_____

_____

_____

_____

_____

_____

_____

_____

_____

_____

_____

_____

_____

CAPÍTULO 9 Tercer paso

Nombre _____ Clase _____ Fecha _____

■ VAMOS A LEER

16 In this chapter, you've learned the names of some specialty stores. You can often figure out what such stores sell by using vocabulary you already know. For example, you can guess that a **frutería** sells **fruta** and that a **panadería** sells **pan**. Below are ads for some other specialty stores. Can you figure out what each one sells or what services it offers? Below each ad, write in English what kind of store you think is being advertised. Reading strategies, such as using pictures and drawings, looking for cognates, and scanning, will help you. Then answer the questions that follow.

CARNICERIA
González

Especialidad en
chorizos, embutidos variados y
cortes de carnes especiales.

Más de 30 años de atención personal

Teléfono 78-4112
Avenida 14 de noviembre 16,
al lado de
la Panadería Continental.

a. _____

CERRAJERIA
MOLINER
con 12 años de experencia
• Instalamos todo tipo de cerradura
• Especialidad en cerraduras
de seguridad

RAPIDO SERVICIO A DOMICILIO
Teléfono: **43-4495**
Calle Lerdo No. 45, Col. Delicias

Servicio 24 horas

b. _____

Droguería
Cepeda, S.A

• Productos farmacéuti-
cos y químicos

• Flores, hierbas y hojas
medicinales

Pedidos:
54-6672 y 54-6675
FAX: 58-0925
Calle Presidente Sur No.
22, Col. Olivar

c. _____

Lavandería **Real**
*Servicio súper rápido con amable
atención personal*
■ **Servicio en menos de 1 hora**
■ **Especializados en ropa fina**
■ **Servicio de lavado y planchado**
■ **Lavado en seco**
*La belleza de su ropa es
nuestro compromiso*
Ubicada en el Centro Comercial
Eurocompras
REPARTO A DOMICILIO
Tels: **74-5567 74-5578 74-5571**

d. _____

Mueblería **La Virreina**

• Surtido completo de muebles finos en
diseños exclusivos
• Electrodomésticos de las mejores marcas
• Precios bajos
• Juegos de sala, comedor,
cocina y recámara
• Facilidades de crédito

TELEFONOS: **34-6771 34-6775**
Calle Ballesteros 63, Apartado 1267

e. _____

Ferretería
Cárdenas, S.A.

**Tenemos todas las
marcas que Ud. desea**

**Tenemos maquinaria
para madera y metal**

**Ferretería especial
e industrial**

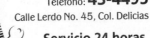

TEL. **88-7093 y 88-7082**
FAX (606) 88-1167

f. _____

---

1. Which store (or stores) do you think might have home delivery service? _____

2. Which store (or stores) might be located in a shopping mall? _____ Why do you think that? _____

3. If you need sauage and bread, where would you probably go? _____ Why? _____

4. You have just moved into a new house, and your parents need to buy new furniture and check on a security system. Which stores will they visit? _____

5. Do any of the stores have round-the-clock service? _____ Which ones? _____

_____

■ CULTURA

17 The following travelers are all in Miami International airport, headed for various Spanish-speaking countries. What currency does each person or group need to get before their flights take off? Hint: Look over the maps on pp. xxi–xxvii of your textbook while doing this activity.

_____ 1. La familia Ybarra va a San Juan.

_____ 2. Daniel Benedetti va a Buenos Aires.

_____ 3. Adela Ramos va a Bogotá.

_____ 4. Beatriz y Felipe Malo van a Quito.

_____ 5. Manolo Hurtado va a Madrid.

_____ 6. Rafael, Karin y Esteban Fajardo van a San José.

_____ 7. Irene Velásquez va a la Ciudad de Guatemala.

_____ 8. Humberto Carranza va al D.F.

_____ 9. Anita Bermúdez va a Caracas.

18 In the **Nota cultural** on p. 240 of your textbook you read about how people in Spain and many other Spanish-speaking countries often do their grocery shopping in specialty stores located in their neighborhoods. They usually buy just enough for one or two days at a time.

a. Now think about how people usually buy groceries where you live. Do they walk to shops near their homes? Do they buy just enough for a few days, or do they buy more?

_____

_____

_____

_____

b. The way you answered question **a.** depends on whether you live in a city or a suburb, a small town, or in the country. Would it be practical to go grocery shopping daily where you live? Why or why not?

_____

_____

_____

_____

10 Celebraciones

■ DE ANTEMANO

1 Everyone's talking while getting ready for a surprise birthday party for Yolanda. Match each of the questions and comments in the first column with the most appropriate response from the second column.

_____ 1. A ver, ¿qué debemos escribir en el pastel?

_____ 2. Oye, Diego. ¿Me ayudas a preparar los tamales?

_____ 3. Rosa, ¿con quién estás hablando?

_____ 4. Y tú, Chuy, ¿qué hiciste?

_____ 5. ¿Sabes quién mandó las invitaciones?

_____ 6. Aquí está el pastel. ¿Qué te parece?

a. Mario. También ayudó a comprar la comida.

b. Con Elena. Quiere saber qué necesita traer a la fiesta.

c. Perfecto. A Yolanda le va a encantar.

d. Pues, limpié la casa y después ayudé a preparar las decoraciones.

e. ¡Claro que sí! ¡Y a comerlos también!

f. Pon "Feliz cumpleaños, Yolanda". ¿Qué más?

2 Look at the **fotonovela**. What word or phrase would you use...?

1. to ask someone what they think of the decorations _____

2. to tell someone that you don't know and that he or she should ask María

_____

3. to tell someone that you'll gladly do what he or she has asked you to do

_____

4. to ask someone what he or she did

_____

5. to say that your sister prepared the food

_____

6. to say that you helped, too

_____

7. to say that you sent out the invitations

_____

8. to ask someone to help you buy the cake

_____

9. to say that you're talking to Beto

_____

■ PRIMER PASO

3 Fill in each calendar page below with the name of the holiday celebrated on that day.

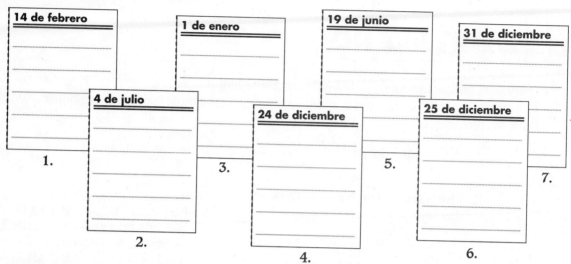

14 de febrero

1. _____

4 de julio

2. _____

1 de enero

24 de diciembre

3. _____

4. _____

19 de junio

5. _____

31 de diciembre

25 de diciembre

6. _____

7. _____

4 Every Sunday, Lupe's Tía Luisa calls from Guadalajara, wanting to know how everyone is and what everybody's doing. Using the cues below and following the model, answer Tía Luisa's questions.

MODELO   TÍA LUISA   ¿Está estudiando Inés? (leer el periódico)
                LUPE   **No, ahora está leyendo el periódico.**

1. ¿Y está lavando el carro Papá? (tomar una siesta)

_____

2. ¿Y Mamá? ¿Está trabajando en el jardín? (hablar con la tía Carmen)

_____

3. ¿Y está Ricardo escribiendo una composición? (leer las tiras cómicas)

_____

4. ¿Están comiendo Sara y Martín? (salir para ir al cine)

_____

5. ¿Y Lourdes? ¿Está corriendo en el parque? (limpiar su cuarto)

_____

6. ¿Y tú? ¿Estás preparando el almuerzo? (ver una película en la televisión)

_____

7. ¿Está Julia lavando los platos? (escuchar música en su cuarto)

_____

8. ¿Y están Toño y Susana bañando al perro? (jugar con sus juguetes)

_____

¡Ven conmigo! Level 1, Chapter 10

5 Every family celebrates holidays in a slightly different way. Pick one holiday you and your family celebrate, and describe what you and your family like to do on that day.

MODELO   **Para el Día de Acción de Gracias, me gusta ir a visitar a mis tíos y primos...**
A mi hermano le gusta ver partidos de fútbol americano en la televisión.

_____

_____

_____

_____

_____

6 **¡Pobre Ana!** She can't make it to her friend Paloma's party because she's sick, but she can't help calling Paloma to find out what's going on. Using the picture below as a guide, write Ana's questions and Paloma's answers. Number 1 is done for you as a model.

1. Bueno, Paloma, ¿qué estás haciendo?
   Estoy sirviendo las galletas en este momento. _____

2. Y Rolando, está allí, ¿no? _____

   _____

3. Se oye música. _____

   _____

4. Y Miguel, está allí con Samuel y Eugenia, ¿verdad? _____

   _____

5. ¿Federico y Roberto? _____

   _____

6. Y la comida, ¿_____ bastante para todos?

HRW material copyrighted under notice appearing earlier in this work.

7 Describe where you are and what you are doing at each of the times below. Use the present progressive.

MODELO   jueves—8:00 P.M.
          Estoy en casa. Estoy mirando mi programa de televisión favorito.

1. lunes—7:00 A.M. _____

2. jueves—12:30 P.M. _____

3. sábado—8:00 A.M. _____

4. viernes—9:30 P.M. _____

5. martes—4:00 P.M. _____

8 Everyone is getting ready for a party. Use the expressions from the **Así se dice** box on p. 264 to create four short conversations between the people in the drawings about who to invite, what food to buy and prepare, and how to decorate the house.

MODELO   — **¿Crees que debemos invitar al director del colegio?**
          — **Sí, buena idea.**

1. — _____
   — _____

2. — _____
   — _____

3. — _____
   — _____

4. — _____
   — _____

■ SEGUNDO PASO

9 Pedro's family is getting ready for a party. He's trying to avoid doing work, but without much success. Create a short conversation for each picture in which Pedro either agrees or politely refuses to do what he's being asked to do, according to the cues.

    1. sí   **2. no**   **3. no**   **4. sí**   **5. sí**

1.   MAMÁ _____

                  _____

       PEDRO _____

                  _____

2.   EVA _____

                  _____

       PEDRO _____

                  _____

3.   PAPÁ _____

                  _____

       PEDRO _____

                  _____

4.   GLORIA _____

                  _____

       PEDRO _____

                  _____

5. ABUELITO _____

                  _____

       PEDRO _____

                  _____

10 Every summer all of Doña Engracia's grandchildren and some of their friends come to spend a couple of weeks with her at the beach. She makes sure things run smoothly by assigning chores to everyone. Write out Doña Engracia's instructions, using informal commands and what you see in each picture below.

MODELO  Tomás
Tomás, saca al perro y compra el periódico, por favor.

1.  Marta

_____

2. Blanca

_____

3.  Armando

_____

4.  Teresa

_____

5. Guillermo

_____

6.  Juan Pablo

_____

7. Victoria

_____

8.  Paloma

_____

9.  Sergio y Mario

_____

¡Ven conmigo! Level 1, Chapter 10

11 Today it's your turn to wash the dishes and clean up the kitchen, but you need to start studying for your Spanish test tomorrow. Write a conversation between you and your brother or sister in which you explain the problem to him or her and ask for help. Your brother or sister should agree to help but should ask you to do a favor for him or her in return.

_____

_____

_____

_____

_____

_____

_____

_____

_____

_____

12 Imagine that you're "King or Queen for a Day" and have a chance to give the orders. Come up with six pieces of advice, recommendations, or instructions for your friends or members of your family, using informal commands of the verbs in parentheses and any other verbs you need.

(poner)

MODELO   **Para mi hermanito: Lava los platos y pon la mesa esta noche.**

1. (poner) _____

_____

2. (hacer) _____

_____

3. (ir) _____

_____

4. (venir) _____

_____

5. (irse) _____

_____

6. (mandar) _____

_____

■ TERCER PASO

13 Carla couldn't go to Consuelo's party last night, so she has called your sister to find out about it. Based on your sister's answers, write the questions Consuelo must be asking on the other end of the telephone line.

MODELO   María Teresa preparó unas empanadas fantásticas.
            ¿Qué preparó María Teresa?

1. Miguel y yo llegamos a las 7:30.

_____

2. Susana llegó a las 8:00 y Marisa llegó a las 10:00.

_____

3. Tomé muchos refrescos.

_____

4. Salvador habló mucho con la chica nueva.

_____

5. María Luisa invitó a Juan a ir al cine.

_____

6. Sí, todos bailamos mucho.

_____

7. Sí, todos lo pasamos muy bien.

_____

8. Terminó a las 11:00.

_____

9. ¡Claro que sí! Ayudé a lavar los platos.

_____

14 Ricardo wanted to get together with some friends yesterday, but no one was around. Looking at the pictures, tell what his friends did yesterday.

1. Carlos y Javi   **2. Sebastián**   **3. Marta, Luz y Ana**   **4. Gustavo y Andrés**   **5. Mis amigos y yo**

1. _____
2. _____
3. _____
4. _____
5. _____

15 Ana had ambitious plans for this week. In her list of things to do she's checked off the things she actually did and made some excuse for each thing that she didn't get around to doing. Using her list, complete the following conversation between Ana and her mother.

> estudiar para el examen ✓ ¡3 HORAS!
> caminar con el perro ✓
> limpiar el cuarto *llamó Gabi*
> ayudar a Juanito con la tarea ✓ ¡Sacó una A!

1. MADRE Ana, ¿estudiaste para el examen de matemáticas?

   ANA _____

2. ANA _____

   MADRE Bueno, no. Es que no hay estampillas.

3. MADRE Y limpiaste tu cuarto, ¿verdad mi amor?

   ANA _____

4. MADRE _____

   ANA Sí, caminamos por todo el parque.

5. MADRE _____

   ANA Sí, ¿y sabes qué? ¡Sacó una A!

16 You and Alfonso are planning the next Spanish Club festival. You've already made a list of assignments for the various tasks that need to be done. Use your list to respond to each of Alfonso's suggestions about who should do each task.

> dibujar el cartel   Laura
> invitar a la directora   Alfonso
> reservar el teatro   Susana
> poner el anuncio en el periódico   Héctor
> organizar el concierto   tú
> escribir el programa   Nelson y Patricia
> decorar el gimnasio   todos nosotros
> tocar la guitarra   Isabel
> preparar la cena   yo

MODELO
ALFONSO ¿Quién va a dibujar el cartel?
TÚ **¿Qué te parece si Laura lo dibuja?**

1. ¿Quién va a tocar la guitarra?

   _____

2. ¿Y quiénes van a decorar el gimnasio?

   _____

3. ¿Quiénes pueden escribir el programa?

_____

4. ¿Quién debe organizar el concierto?

_____

5. ¿Quién va a poner el anuncio *(ad)* en el periódico?

_____

6. ¿Quién puede preparar la cena?

_____

7. ¿Quién va a invitar a la directora *(principal)*?

_____

8. ¿Quién debe reservar el teatro?

_____

17 Using the verbs in the box, or other **-ar** verbs you know, write a series of sentences describing something you and your friends did at the indicated time.

| preparar | invitar |
| mandar | llamar |

1. (day before yesterday) ¿Quién llamó al profesor de español? (Sergio)

_____

2. (last Saturday) ¿Quiénes hicieron la tortilla española? (Marcos y Graciela)

_____

3. (last summer) ¿Quién compró el helado? (Ricardo)

_____

4. (last year) ¿Quién decoró la sala? (La hermana de Ernesto)

_____

5. (in 1995) ¿Quiénes tocaron la guitarra? (Cristina y Éster)

_____

6. (last night)

_____

7. (yesterday)

_____

■ VAMOS A LEER

18 One of the biggest yearly celebrations for many Spanish-speaking communities happens during **Semana Santa**, or *Holy Week*. The best-known **Semana Santa** celebrations take place in Seville, Spain. People come from all over to watch the solemn, majestic processions move through Seville's narrow, twisted streets. The city of Tandil, in Argentina, also has Holy Week festivities as described in the program below.

Semana Santa
Programa de Actos Extraordinarios

SABADO 26 DE MARZO
19.30 hs.: Inauguración del XVIII Salón de Arte Sacro – Museo Municipal de Bellas Artes – Chacabuco 357
21.00 hs.: Misa Criolla – Peña Antonio J. Hernet, de la Sociedad de Fomento La Esperanza – Teatro Estrada – Fuerte Independencia 354 – Entrada A 4.

DOMINGO 27 DE MARZO
18.00 hs.: Circuito Cultural de Verano – Plaza Independencia – Banda Municipal, conjuntos, solistas.
21.00 hs.: Misa Criolla – Peña Antonio J. Hernet, de la Sociedad de Fomento La Esperanza – Teatro Estrada – Fuerte Independencia 354 – Entrada A 4.

LUNES 28 DE MARZO
19.00 hs.: Plaza Independencia: Banda Muncipal y Ballet Infantil – En caso de lluvia se realiza en Teatro Estrada – Fuerte Independencia 354

MARTES 29 DE MARZO
22.00 hs.: Via Crucis (Jornada Sacra) de Helvio I. Botana – Teatro leído por la Comedia Tandilense – Dirección: José María Guimet – Auditorium Municipal, entrada libre.

MIERCOLES 30 DE MARZO
19.00 hs.: Plaza Independencia: Banda Municipal y conjuntos folklóricos. En caso de lluvia se realiza en Teatro Estrada, Fuerte Independencia 354.

JUEVES 31 DE MARZO
21.30 hs.: Auditorium Municipal: Canto por la Paz, con Carlos Mansilla – Las Voces de Aymará – Relatos: A. Maschio, con la participación de Roberto Gómez y J.C. Etcheverre – Entrada A 4.

21.00 hs.: Escenas de la Redención (Dirección: José María Guimet) – Anfiteatro Municipal (al pie del Parque Independencia) – Entrada A 4.

VIERNES 1 DE ABRIL
17.30 hs.: Via Crucis en el Monte Clavario – Monseñor de Andrea al 400.
18.30 hs.: Solemne Procesión del Viernes Santo.
21.00 hs.: Escenas de la Redención en el Anfiteatro Municipal.

SABADO 2 DE ABRIL
19.00 hs.: Cantata No. 4 de Johann S. Bach – Concierto Sinfónico Coral por la Orquesta de Cámara de Olavarría y Coro Estable de Tandil – Teatro Estrada Entrada A 5.
21.30 hs.: Canto por la Paz – Auditorium Municipal – Entrada A 4.
21.00 hs.: Escenas de la Redención – Anfiteatro Municipal – Cnel. Dorrego y Judain.

DOMINGO 3 DE ABRIL
17 a 21 hs.: Espectáculos artísticos en la Feria de los Artesanos – Diagonal Parque Independencia.
19.00 hs.: Conjunto Municipal de Bandoneones Dirección: Norberto Matti – Teatro Estrada – Entrada A 4.
21.00 hs.: Escenas de la Redención en el Anfiteatro Municipal.

JUEVES A DOMINGO
Feria Artesanal en la Diagonal Sarmiento, acceso Parque Independencia. Feria de Artesanías Latinoamericana. Centro Polivalente de Arte – Pinto y Alem.

"Semana Santa 1988: Programa de Actos Extraordinarios" from brochure, *Semana Santa en Tandil: Programación oficial y no oficial 1988.* Reprinted by permission of ***Dirección Municipal de Turismo, Argentina.***

1. Are there events scheduled for every day during **Semana Santa**?

_____

2. What are some of the types of events scheduled this week?

_____

3. Can you find any references to religious events?

_____

4. Suppose that you want to go to the performance given on Monday by the **Banda Municipal y Ballet Infantil**. At what time is the performance and where is it being given? Where will it be held in case of rain?

_____

_____

◼ CULTURA

19 Saint's days, celebrated throughout the Spanish-speaking world, are associated with each day of the year. Special calendars called **santorales** show which saint is honored on that day. Children may be named for the saint on whose day they were born. For example, a boy born on April 3, the day of Saint Richard, could be named Ricardo. Below is the month of April taken from a **santoral**. Look it over, then answer the questions.

DOM	LUN	MAR	MIER	JUE	VIER	SAB
				1 San Melitón	2 Sta. Ofelia	3 San Ricardo
4 D. de Ramos	5 Sta. Emilia	6 San Celso	7 San Donato	8 Jueves Santo	9 Viernes Santo	10 Sábado Santo
11 D. de Pascua	12 San Damián	13 San Hermenegildo	14 San Valeriano	15 Sta. Anastasia	16 Sta. Engracia	17 San Aniceto
18 San Perfecto	19 San Crescencio	20 San Sulpicio	21 San Anselmo	22 San Sotero	23 San Jorge	24 San Alejandro
25 San Marcos	26 San Cleto	27 Sta. Zita	28 San Prudencio	29 Sta. Catalina de S.	30 Día del Niño	

1. When in April will your friend Marcos celebrate his saint's day?

_____

2. A couple had a baby girl in January and decided to name her Emilia after her grandmother. When will Emilia celebrate her saint's day?

_____

3. If a baby boy is born on April 21, what might his parents choose to name him?

_____

4. One of your friends was born on April 23 and was named after the saint honored on that day. What is his name?

_____

_____

5. Your friend has a crush on a classmate of yours named Ofelia. When in April would be a good day for your friend to leave Ofelia a card in her locker? Why?

_____

_____

11 Para vivir bien

■ DE ANTEMANO

1 Match each of the following questions with the most appropriate response.

_____ 1. Oye, ¿por qué no descansamos un poco aquí en esta banca?

_____ 2. ¿Ustedes van al Museo Pablo Casals? ¡Yo también!

_____ 3. ¿Tienes ganas de patinar sobre ruedas conmigo esta tarde?

_____ 4. ¿Qué tal si vamos a la Plaza de Hostos esta mañana?

_____ 5. ¿Adónde fueron hoy?

a. No, gracias. Es que no me siento muy bien.

b. ¿Sí? Entonces, ¿por qué no vas con nosotros?

c. Al Castillo del Morro. Debes ir allí también, porque es muy interesante.

d. ¡Buena idea! Estoy cansado y además me duelen mucho los pies.

e. Bueno, fuimos allí ayer. ¿Por qué no vamos a la Fortaleza?

2 In the **fotonovela**, Ben, Carmen, and Pedro talk about where they went and what they did during their day in Old San Juan. Where have you gone lately? Complete the sentences below.

MODELO Anoche fui *(I went)* a...
Anoche fui a la casa de mi amigo Greg para estudiar.

1. El mes pasado fui a...

_____

2. El fin de semana pasado fui a...

_____

3. Ayer después de clases fui a...

_____

4. Anoche después de cenar fui a...

_____

5. Esta mañana fui a...

_____

6. Antes de la clase de español hoy, fui a...

_____

■ PRIMER PASO

3 You're on your school's baseball team and tomorrow's the big championship game. Write sentences saying how each of the following people feel before the big game.

MODELO   Yolanda/mal

Yolanda se siente mal.

1. Julio/cansado _____

2. Tú/muy bien _____

3. Ricardo/un poco mal _____

4. El entrenador *(coach)*/nervioso _____

5. Yo/magnífico/a _____

6. Alicia/muy confidente _____

4 For each situation below, ask the person in the picture how she or he feels or make a suggestion. Then write the response each person or pair might make. Use expressions and vocabulary from pages 291–292 of your textbook.

feliz	*happy*
triste	*sad*
horrible	*awful*

MODELO   

Tú: ¿Qué tienes?

Alejandra: **Me siento muy cansada.**

Alejandra

Guillermo   **Teresa**   **Mónica**   **José Luis y Margarita**   **Enrique y Paloma**

1.   Tú: _____

    Guillermo: _____

2.   Tú: _____

    Teresa: _____

3.   Tú: _____

    Mónica: _____

4.   Tú: _____

    José Luis: _____

    Margarita: _____

5.   Tú: _____

    Enrique: _____

    Paloma: _____

¡Ven conmigo! Level 1, Chapter 11

5 Everyone's making plans for after school on the bus ride home. Can you match each invitation to its correct response?

1. _____
¿Qué tal si patinamos sobre ruedas esta tarde?

a.
No, ya me siento bien. Sí, vamos... ¡quiero ver esa nueva película de aventuras!

2. _____
¿Por qué no hacemos yoga en el gimnasio a las cuatro?

b.
Yo sí voy, pero creo que Tomás no va a ir. Se siente mal hoy.

3. _____
¿Quieres ir al cine esta tarde, o todavía te sientes mal?

c.
Nada, estoy bien. Nada más tengo que estirarme primero para no lastimarme los músculos.

4. _____
¿Por qué no van Uds. al partido de béisbol conmigo?

d.
Hoy me siento un poco cansado. Tal vez podemos hacer ejercicio mañana.

5. _____
¿Por qué no quieres levantar pesas conmigo? ¿Qué tienes?

e.
Gracias, pero no me siento bien hoy. No tengo ganas de patinar.

6 Imagine that you're a fitness trainer and that you work in a sports club. What kind of suggestions would you give to each of the following clients based on what they tell you? Use the new vocabulary on p. 292 of your textbook, as well as sports vocabulary you learned in earlier chapters. In the box are some other possibilities.

el alpinismo	*rock climbing/mountain climbing*
las artes marciales	*martial arts*
el ciclismo	*cycling*
la equitación	*horseback riding*
el esquí acuático/alpino	*water skiing/downhill skiing*
el esquí de travesía	*cross-country skiing*
el footing	*jogging, running*
el patinaje sobre hielo	*ice skating*
la tabla de vela	*windsurfing*

MODELO   Me encanta estar en la playa. ¿Qué tipo de ejercicio puedo hacer?
Bueno, ¿por qué no practicas el esquí acuático? Y también puedes hacer el footing.

1. Quiero practicar algún deporte, pero sólo me gustan los deportes solitarios.

   _____

   _____

2. No me gusta el ejercicio, pero sí me gusta escuchar música.

   _____

   _____

3. Prefiero hacer ejercicio con otras personas.

   _____

   _____

4. No me gusta hacer ejercicio cuando hace calor. Prefiero el frío.

   _____

   _____

5. No quiero ir a un gimnasio. Me gusta más estar afuera, en contacto con la naturaleza *(nature)*.

   _____

   _____

6. Prefiero hacer ejercicio adentro *(inside)*.

   _____

   _____

7. Tengo muchas presiones *(pressure)* y estrés en mi vida. ¿Cómo puedo llevar una vida más sana?

   _____

   _____

8. No me siento bien después de levantar pesas o correr.

   _____

   _____

■ SEGUNDO PASO

7 Write a question asking each person or group pictured how she or he is feeling or what the matter is. Then write each person's answer to your question, using the expressions on p. 294 of your textbook. Then explain why each person feels that way.

MODELO  ¿Por qué están preocupadas ustedes?
Estamos preocupadas porque una amiga está enferma.

1. Blanca

¿_____?

_____

2. Alonso

¿_____?

_____

3. Marcos

¿_____?

_____

4. El Sr. Villalobos

¿_____?

_____

5. Begoña

¿_____?

_____

6. Arturo

¿_____?

_____

7. Francisco y Bernardo

¿_____?

_____

8. Fernando y Celia

¿_____?

_____

8 We all feel different emotions in various situations. For example, you might love the idea of going skydiving, while your best friend would be scared stiff. Complete the questionnaire below about how you feel in different situations.

MODELO   Estoy feliz...
          Estoy feliz cuando salgo con mis amigos los viernes por la noche.

*E*stoy histérico(a) cuando..._____

*M*e da asco° cuando como..._____

*E*stoy preocupado(a) cuando..._____

*E*stoy nervioso(a) cuando..._____

*E*stoy triste cuando..._____

*E*stoy feliz cuando..._____

Mis emociones

Me da asco.   *It grosses me out.*

9 To test her biology class, Sra. Robles gave her students this quiz on anatomy. Can you fill in the missing words from the drawing below? The first one is done for you as an example.

a. el pelo

b. _____

c. _____

d. _____

e. _____

f. _____

g. _____

h. _____

i. _____

j. _____

k. _____

l. _____

m. _____

n. _____

o. _____

p. _____

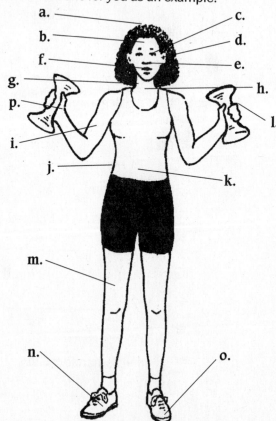

HRW material copyrighted under notice appearing earlier in this work.

10 Your school's hiking club just got back from a weekend excursion and a lot of people have minor aches and pains. Look at the drawings. Then describe what's wrong with each person and explain what they did or what condition they have that caused the problem.

MODELO Claudia
A Claudia le duelen los pies. Patinó sobre ruedas por muchas horas.

jugar al fútbol estar resfriado
levantar 20 kgs. tener gripe
caminar sin zapatos
estirarse   comer
escribir a máquina mucha
por 3 horas   pizza

1. Sergio _____
_____
_____

2. La Profesora Aguilar
_____
_____

3. Tú
_____
_____
_____

4. Elena
_____
_____

5. Daniel
_____
_____

6. Yo
_____
_____

7. Laura
_____
_____

8. Miguel y Fátima
_____
_____

HRW material copyrighted under notice appearing earlier in this work.

■ TERCER PASO

11 Débora is trying to convince her friend Sebastián that most of their friends are athletic. What would Débora say to explain where each person or group of people went and what they did this last weekend, according to the pictures. Use the verbs **ir**, **jugar**, or other verbs in the preterite.

1. Débora (yo)

_____

_____

2. Sebastián (tú)

_____

_____

3. Tú y yo

_____

_____

4. Carlos y Juanita

_____

_____

5. Rogelio e Iván

_____

_____

6. Diego y sus amigos

_____

_____

7. Patricia

_____

_____

8. César

_____

_____

12 When Sra. Castañeda gets home from work, she always wants to know where everyone went and what they did that day. Following the model below and the cues in parentheses, write out Sra. Castañeda's questions and her son Nicolás's answers.

MODELO   abuelo

SRA. CASTAÑEDA   ¿Adónde fue abuelo?
NICOLÁS   **Fue a la panadería y compró unos panes dulces bastante ricos.**

1. tus hermanas

SRA. CASTAÑEDA _____

NICOLÁS _____

_____

_____

2. papá

SRA. CASTAÑEDA _____

NICOLÁS _____

_____

_____

3. tú

SRA. CASTAÑEDA _____

NICOLÁS _____

_____

_____

4. Rodrigo y su amigo

SRA. CASTAÑEDA _____

NICOLÁS _____

_____

_____

5. el perro Sultán

SRA. CASTAÑEDA _____

NICOLÁS _____

_____

_____

13 As you read in the **Sugerencia** on p. 302 of your textbook, using a Spanish-English dictionary can be tricky, especially when words have more than one meaning. For example, let's say you forgot how to say *tennis court*, so you look up *court* in the dictionary. But what do you find?

a. At first this listing may seem confusing, but by reading through it, you can figure out that Spanish translations of *court* are separated according to different meanings. For example, a *tennis court*, a *law court*, and a *royal court* all have different words in Spanish. What are they?

_____

If you read through the whole entry, you'll also see that *court* can be used as a noun or a verb in Spanish, just as in English. When you use a Spanish-English dictionary, make sure you know how you want to use the word and what part of speech it is. Otherwise, you might end up saying something pretty funny, like the person below!

> **court** [kɔːt] **1** *n* **(a)** (*Archit*) patio *m*; (*large room*) sala *f*.
> **(b)** (*Sport*) pista *f*, cancha *f*; **hard** — pista *f* dura.
> **(c)** (*royal*) corte *f*; **at** — en la corte; — **circular** noticiario *m* de la corte.
> **(d) to pay** — to hacer la corte a.
> **(e)** (*Law*) tribunal *m*, juzgado *m*; divorce — tribunal *m* de pleitos matrimoniales; **high** —, **supreme** — tribunal *m* supremo; **juvenile** — tribunal *m* tutelar de menores; **police** — tribunal *m* de policía; — **of appeal** tribunal *m* de casación; — **of inquiry** comisión *f* de investigación; — **of justice** tribunal *m* de justicia; **in open** — en pleno tribunal; **to laugh something out of** — rechazar algo poniéndolo en ridículo; **to rule something out of** — no admitir algo; **to settle out of** — arreglar una disputa de modo privado; **to take someone to** — demandar a uno; recurrir a la vía judicial.
> **2** *vt woman* cortejar, hacer la corte a, (*less formally*) tener relaciones con; *favour* solicitar; *danger, trouble* buscar; *disaster* correr a.
> **3** *vi* estar en relaciones, ser novios; **they've been —ing 3 years** llevan 3 años de relaciones; **are you —ing?** ¿tienes novio?; **—ing couple** pareja *f* de novios.

Excerpt from *Collins Spanish-English, English-Spanish Dictionary* by Colin Smith in collaboration with Manuel Bermejo Marcos and Eugenio Chang-Rodriguez. Copyright © 1971 by William Collins Sons & Co. Ltd. Reprinted by permission of **HarperCollins Publishers UK.**

Jugamos tenis en la corte ayer.

b. Using a good Spanish-English dictionary, look up the following words: *play, back,* and *track.* Can you find different meanings and usages for each word?

_____

_____

_____

14 Write a paragraph explaining several places where you and your friends and relatives went each day last week. What did each of you do there?

_____

_____

_____

_____

_____

_____

■ VAMOS A LEER

15 Have you ever had mint tea to settle an upset stomach, or steaming hot lemon tea for a sore throat? Remedies such as these are very popular in the Spanish-speaking world. People suffering from mild ailments can buy mixtures of **plantas medicinales**, or *medicinal herbs*, at **yerberías**, open-air markets and pharmacies. The teas made from these herbs, called **infusiones**, are specially blended for different health problems.

Read through the descriptions of four **infusiones** below, then answer the questions.

Laboratorios
Saluflor, S.A.

Plantas medicinales **NATURA VITA**

NATURA VITA N° 5 DESCONGESTIVO RESPIRATORIO
Indicado en bronquitis, enfermedades pulmonares, resfriados y gripes. Tomada regularmente se evitan resfriados y aumenta las defensas del sistema respiratorio.

NATURA VITA N° 8 DIGESTIVO
Indicado en dolores de estómago, acidez y falta de apetito. Contribuye a mejorar la digestión.

NATURA VITA N° 11 CALMANTE Y TRANQUILIZANTE
Indicado en estados de estrés y ansiedad. Facilita un sueño natural y profundo. No crea dependencia.

NATURA VITA N° 13 ANTIRREUMATICA
Indicado en artritis, artrosis y problemas reumáticos en general.

CAPÍTULO 11 Vamos a leer

Look at the words that appear in capital letters at the beginning of each description. Based on what you've read, which herbal tea do you think the pharmacy clerk might recommend to each of the following people?

_____ 1. Sra. Vasconcelos has a high-pressure job and can't seem to relax.

_____ 2. Don Luis, 90 years old, is in pretty good shape, but when it rains his bones and joints ache.

_____ 3. Sr. Guzmán sometimes eats too quickly and gets bad stomach aches.

_____ 4. Luisa went outside without her raincoat on Tuesday and now she's got a cold.

■ CULTURA

16 **Yerba mate** is a tea that is enjoyed widely in South America. People typically drink **mate** through a metal straw, called a **bombilla**, from a hollowed-out gourd. Read the advertisement for **mate** below.

EL MATE ES TU AMIGO FIEL

La yerba mate es una extraordinaria bebida natural. Es como un amigo, un amigo fiel que comparte lo mejor de tu vida. Frío o caliente, éstos son algunos de los beneficios saludables de la yerba mate:

✔ *Es dietético.*
✔ *Vence al calor o al frío.*
✔ *Facilita la recuperación física.*

✔ *Mejora la digestión.*
✔ *Tiene un sabor rico.*
✔ *Disminuye el estrés.*

Which of the following benefits are claimed by the ad for **mate**? Check all that apply. Can you imagine any undesirable effects a stimulant tea might have?

1. _____ helps you recuperate physically

2. _____ gives you energy

3. _____ helps with insomnia

4. _____ tastes great

5. _____ helps with digestive problems

6. _____ lowers stress and tension

7. _____ helps with depression

8. _____ helps you if you're dieting

17 As you read in the **Nota cultural** on p. 298 of your textbook, baseball is popular in Caribbean rim countries. Besides following U.S. teams, these countries have formed leagues of their own. Along with the sport, Spanish has imported many baseball-related words from English, starting with **béisbol**. The headlines and captions below show how similar Spanish and English are when it comes to this sport.

Canseco batea su 26to. jonrón del año

21er jonrón de Rafael Palmeiro

Lanza Hinojosa juego de un hit

Ponen out a Morelos en inning 11

Look over the list of Spanish and English baseball vocabulary below. Can you match each Spanish word to its English equivalent?

_____ 1. picheo

_____ 2. ampáyer

_____ 3. doble juego

_____ 4. batear

_____ 5. jonrón

_____ 6. base

_____ 7. liga

_____ 8. doblete

_____ 9. triplete

a. home run
b. triple
c. league
d. pitching
e. umpire
f. double
g. to bat
h. double-header
i. base

CAPÍTULO

12 Las vacaciones ideales

■ DE ANTEMANO

1 Imagine that you are touring Puerto Rico and have a free day in San Juan. Starting out at the **Plaza de Colón**, you figure that you have enough time to see five attractions before meeting up with friends at **El Morro**. Looking at the map of Old San Juan, write a postcard to your friends and suggest an itinerary, including five things you would like to see and do. Include the expressions **¿Por qué no...?** and **¿Qué tal si...?** in your suggestions.

MODELO   **A mí me gustaría ver el Museo del Mar. ¿Por qué no vamos allí primero. Después, ¿qué tal si...? Y luego...**

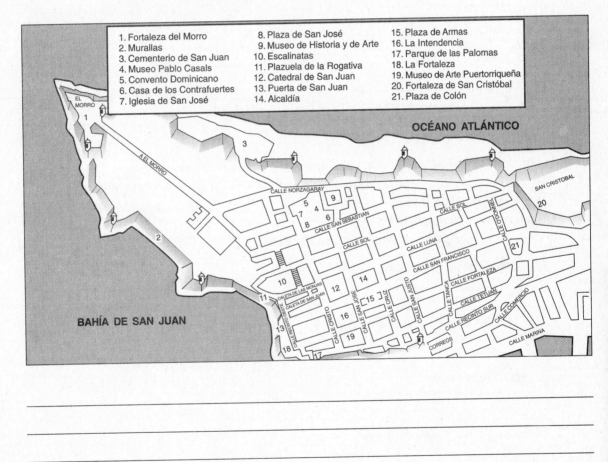

1. Fortaleza del Morro
2. Murallas
3. Cementerio de San Juan
4. Museo Pablo Casals
5. Convento Dominicano
6. Casa de los Contrafuertes
7. Iglesia de San José
8. Plaza de San José
9. Museo de Historia y de Arte
10. Escalinatas
11. Plazuela de la Rogativa
12. Catedral de San Juan
13. Puerta de San Juan
14. Alcaldía
15. Plaza de Armas
16. La Intendencia
17. Parque de las Palomas
18. La Fortaleza
19. Museo de Arte Puertorriqueña
20. Fortaleza de San Cristóbal
21. Plaza de Colón

_____
_____
_____
_____
_____
_____
_____
_____

CAPÍTULO 12 De antemano

■ PRIMER PASO

2 How much does your daily routine change when school's out? Make a list below of four things you do regularly during the school year. Then say how often you do them during the summer. Use the expressions from the box.

muchas veces   a veces
nunca   todos los...
siempre   todos los días

MODELO   hacer la tarea
Por lo general, hago la tarea casi todos los días. ¡Pero durante el verano, no la hago nunca!

1. _____

_____

2. _____

_____

3. _____

_____

4. _____

_____

3 Everyone in study hall today is daydreaming about summer vacation. Explain what each person's plans are using the cues and following the model. If you need help with the forms of the verbs, see p. 318 of your textbook.

preferir   (no) querer
(no) tener ganas de

MODELO   Adriana/ir a Puerto Rico.
Adriana quiere ir a Puerto Rico.

1. Raúl/visitar a sus primos

_____

2. Susana y Juanita/ir a Nueva York

_____

3. Yo/ir a California

_____

4. La profesora/viajar a México

_____

5. Isa y Ramón/ir a Miami

_____

6. Todos nosotros/descansar

_____

4 Everyone's going somewhere this summer! Write a question asking where the following people are planning to go, then write a response including what they'll do there. Use the expressions in the **Así se dice** box on p. 318 of your textbook, your imagination, and what you've learned about each destination.

MODELO   Lourdes/San Antonio, Texas
                  Lourdes, ¿adónde vas a viajar este verano?
                  Voy a San Antonio. Allí quiero visitar a mis primos y ver el Paseo del Río.

1. José Luis/Quito, Ecuador

   _____

   _____

2. Ernesto y Cristina/San Juan, Puerto Rico

   _____

   _____

3. Óscar y yo/Cuernavaca, México

   _____

   _____

4. El director del colegio/Madrid, España

   _____

   _____

5. Sara y Paloma/Miami, Florida

   _____

   _____

5 Now it's your turn to talk about summer plans. Write two sentences explaining what each of the people or groups of people listed below are planning for summer, using the expressions from the **Así se dice** box on p. 318 of your textbook.

MODELO   mis primos
                  Este verano, mis primos piensan hacer un viaje al Gran Cañón. Van
                  a estar allí por dos semanas.

1. yo _____

   _____

2. mis hermanos _____

   _____

3. mi mejor amigo/a _____

   _____

CAPÍTULO 12 Primer paso

4. el/la profesor/a _____

_____

5. mis compañeros de clase _____

_____

6. mis vecinos *(neighbors)* _____

_____

6 Look at the pictures of the places that the people below are planning on going to for vacation. Write a sentence describing the weather there, then mention three things that each person or group of people will need to take with them, using the **Vocabulario** on p. 319 and other clothing vocabulary from Chapter 9.

Herlinda

1. _____

_____

Joaquín y Pilar

2. _____

_____

Luis y David

3. _____

_____

La familia Dávila

4. _____

_____

María

5. _____

_____

Norma y Gabriela

6. _____

_____

■ SEGUNDO PASO

7 One night at dinner, Raquel and her family began talking about their dream vacations. Complete Raquel's description of her family's opinions using the new words on p. 322 of your textbook. Do her family's ideas of the perfect vacation sound like yours?

¿Cuáles son nuestras vacaciones ideales? Pues... depende de la persona. A mí me gustaría

1. _____ el río Colorado en 2. _____ y ver el Gran Cañón desde el río. A

mi hermano le gustaría 3. _____ la selva tropical del Brasil. Mi padre prefiere

4. _____. Pero a mi madre le encanta la idea de 5. _____ en todas las

grandes ciudades europeas, como Madrid, París y Londres. ¿Y mis abuelos? Pues, a mi abuela le

gustaría 6. _____ las Montañas Rocosas en Colorado. Por su parte, mi abuelo prefiere

7. _____ en el Parque Nacional de Yellowstone. ¡Qué familia tan complicada!

8 Everyone's studying for the final exam in Spanish, but they all take a few minutes to think about what they'd rather be doing! In Item 1, write a question asking what Damián and his friends would like to do. Then in Items 2–5, write the answers Damián would give about himself and each of his friends.

| 1. Damián | 2. Silvia | 3. Eugenio | 4. Rosa | 5. Maricarmen |

1. _____

   _____

2. _____

   _____

3. _____

   _____

4. _____

   _____

5. _____

CAPÍTULO 12 Segundo paso

9 Look over the **Gramática** section on p. 325. Would you use **ser** or **estar** in each of the situations below? Explain which verb you would use and why.

1. to ask your mom where your jacket is _____

2. to ask a friend why he or she's so upset _____

3. to tell someone on the bus the time _____

4. to describe your little brother or sister _____

5. to find out who the person at your friend's party is _____

6. to tell your teacher where your homework is _____

7. to describe the great sweater your parents got you for your birthday

_____

8. to tell the doctor how you are feeling _____

10 Lupe is at the beach writing a letter to her cousin Jesús back home in San Antonio. Complete the letter with the correct form of **ser** or **estar**. If you need help deciding which verb to use, look over the **Gramática** box on p. 325 of your textbook.

> Querido Jesús,
>
> ¡Saludos desde la playa! Aquí 1. _____ (yo) en Puerto Dorado. ¡Este lugar 2. _____ increíble! La playa 3. _____ preciosa y muy grande.
>
> No 4. _____ (nosotros) aburridos para nada, porque hay muchísimas cosas que hacer. Por ejemplo, hoy Sara y José 5. _____ aprendiendo a saltar en paracaídas. Y yo 6. _____ tomando clases de tabla vela°.
>
> Hay unos muchachos aquí que también 7. _____ de San Antonio. 8. _____ muy simpáticos, y todos vamos a salir esta noche a bailar.
>
> Ahora 9. _____ las doce y media. Hace sol y calor. A la una, vamos a almorzar a un café que 10. _____ muy cerca de nuestro hotel. La comida aquí 11. _____ riquísima.
>
> Bueno, es todo por ahora. 12. _____ (yo) un poco cansada porque caminé con Sara esta mañana por la playa. ¡Caminamos cuatro millas y ahora me duelen las piernas!
>
> Espero que estés bien. ¡Saludos a todos!
>
> Un beso,
>
> Lupe

tabla vela *windsurfing*

HRW material copyrighted under notice appearing earlier in this work.

11 Diana and Gustavo have one more test to go before vacation begins. Write out a dialogue between them based on the cues below. If you're unsure of whether to use **ser** or **estar**, refer to p. 325 of your textbook.

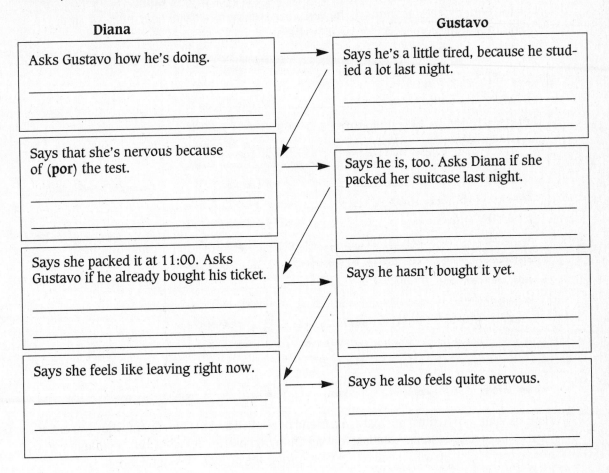

Diana

Asks Gustavo how he's doing.

_____

_____

Says that she's nervous because of (**por**) the test.

_____

_____

Says she packed it at 11:00. Asks Gustavo if he already bought his ticket.

_____

_____

Says she feels like leaving right now.

_____

_____

Gustavo

Says he's a little tired, because he studied a lot last night.

_____

_____

Says he is, too. Asks Diana if she packed her suitcase last night.

_____

_____

Says he hasn't bought it yet.

_____

_____

Says he also feels quite nervous.

_____

_____

12 You and a group of friends are trying to plan a trip this summer. Everyone has a different idea about where to go and what to do. Choose your favorite activity from those on p. 322 of your textbook (or another activity you like) and try to convince your friends to join you. Write a short paragraph explaining where you want to go, what you want to do, and why.

MODELO   **Creo que debemos ir al Parque Yosemite para acampar porque...**

_____

_____

_____

_____

_____

_____

_____

CAPÍTULO 12 Segundo paso

■ TERCER PASO

13 Below is a postcard from Carmen to one of her friends in New York. Complete the postcard using the correct preterite forms of the verbs in parentheses. If you need help with the preterite verb forms, see p. 327 of your textbook.

Querida Tamara,

¡Hola! Nosotros 1. (llegar) _____ a Puerto Rico la semana pasada y lo estamos pasando muy bien. El fin de semana pasado Ben y yo 2. (ir) _____ a la capital e 3. (hacer) _____ un recorrido por Viejo San Juan. Nosotros 4. (visitar) _____ el Museo Casals y El Morro. Yo 5. (comprar) _____ unos regalos también. ¡Nosotros 6. (caminar) _____ mucho ese día! Ayer mamá nos 7. (llevar) _____ al bosque tropical, El Yunque. ¡Es increíble! Allí yo 8. (escalar) _____ una montaña con Ben y nosotros 9. (explorar) _____ el bosque. Mamá 10. (sacar) _____ muchas fotos de nosotros. Y esta tarde 11. (jugar) _____ al béisbol con mi tío y mis primos. Bueno, me despido. Nos vemos pronto.

Un beso,
Carmen

Tamara Santander
623 W. 125th St., # 3B
New York, NY 10012

14 Now it's your turn. Write a postcard to a friend or relative and tell him or her what you did on vacation. You can describe your last real vacation or make up details about an imaginary one. If you need help with the preterite verb forms, see p. 327 of your textbook.

CAPÍTULO 12 Tercer paso

15 Imagine that you're a friend of Arturo, who is illustrated below. In item 1, ask him where he and his classmates went last summer and what they did there. The, in items 2–8, write Arturo's answers.

1. _____
   _____
   _____

La clase de español

2. _____
   _____

Esteban, Emilia y Rogelio

3. _____
   _____

Arturo

4. _____
   _____

Juan Carlos, Norberto y Elena

5. _____
   _____

Diego y Guillermo

6. _____
   _____

Sonia y Rubén

7. _____
   _____

Los Alvarado

8. _____
   _____

CAPÍTULO 12 Tercer paso

16 There's been a computer problem at the travel agency, and now the plane tickets have gotten mixed up. Help sort out which ticket is for whom. Read what each person says about his or her trip and figure out which ticket is for him or her. Write the person's name on the right ticket.

Carolina

Voy a escalar montañas en los Alpes con mis amigos Ulrike y Klaus.

Nombre: _____

Destino: Inglaterra

El profesor Valdés

Soy profesor de arqueología. Voy a investigar las pirámides.

Nombre: _____

Destino: Argentina

Rosaura

Voy a hacer un recorrido por Pekín y Shanghai. Y tengo ganas de ver la Gran Muralla (Great Wall).

Nombre: _____

Destino: Alemania

Fernando

Este verano voy a hacer un cursillo de francés y estudiar arte en el Museo del Louvre.

Nombre: _____

Destino: Costa Rica

La profesora Iturbe

Este verano mi marido y yo vamos a bajar el río Amazonas y explorar la selva.

Nombre: _____

Destino: Italia

Enrique

Voy a estudiar inglés y quedarme con (stay with) una familia inglesa. ¡Voy a estar allí dos meses y seguro que voy a aprender mucho!

Nombre: _____

Destino: China

El Sr. Carvajal

Tengo que hacer un viaje a Milán para mis negocios. Pero también espero hacer un poco de turismo.

Nombre: _____

Destino: Egipto

Victoria

Voy a visitar a unos primos en Buenos Aires. Espero tener tiempo para unas excursiones, porque me gustaría ver los Andes.

Nombre: _____

Destino: Francia

Nombre: _____

Destino: Brasil

CAPÍTULO 12 Tercer paso

■ VAMOS A LEER

17 Below is a brochure describing a summer camp program in Spain. Look over the brochure, then answer the questions.

Campamento de verano
San Martín del Pinar   *desde 1978*

Lugar Campamento San Martín del Pinar, ubicado cerca de Jaca (Huesca), al pie de los Pirineos. Nuestro campamento cuenta con comedor cubierto, enfermería, servicios y duchas de agua caliente y fría, piscina, canchas de tenis y de fútbol, pista de correr, picadero de caballos y un río donde realizar diversas actividades acuáticas.
Fecha 10 de julio al 30 de agosto.
Participantes Niños y jóvenes entre los 8 y los 16 años.
Metodología
• Actividades según grupos de edad.
• Hay un monitor por cada 10 participantes.

• Responsables jóvenes monitores, con formación en educación física, artes y sicología.
• Programa y entrenamiento reconocidos por las Comunidades Autónomas.
Actividades
Gran variedad de actividades deportivas y recreativas, natación, equitación, tiro con arco, fuegos de campamento, excursiones y marchas, clases de inglés con monitores norteamericanos y mucho más.
Importe 56.000 Ptas. por dos semanas
El importe incluye...
Transporte en autobús desde Barcelona y regreso, comida, desayuno, merienda, cena, alojamiento en tiendas, material de actividades, supervisión continua de monitores, transporte durante las excursiones y servicios de enfermería.
Plazo de inscripción Hasta el 20 de junio
Para mayor información
   Viajes Euro-Ibéricos, S.A.
   C/. Leñeros, 61
   34022 Madrid
   O llame al **(91) 556 78 43/77 21**

1. Where is the camp located? What are three things the brochure mentions about the place?

_____

_____

2. What is the age group of the campers? _____

3. Look over the activities offered. You should recognize some of the words in this section. Can you use context and cognates to guess the meaning of the following? Match each word with its English equivalent.

_____ 1. monitores   a. *hikes*

_____ 2. equitación   b. *archery*

_____ 3. fuegos de campamento   c. *instructors/counselors*

_____ 4. marchas   d. *horseback riding*

_____ 5. tiro con arco   e. *campfires*

4. If you could go to the perfect summer camp, where would it be and what would you do? Write a description of the ideal summer camp, using the brochure above as a model. Include details about location, campers, activities, sports, and recreation.

_____

_____

_____

_____

_____

CAPÍTULO 12 Vamos a leer

◼ CULTURA

18 In many parts of the Spanish-speaking world, students go on **excursiones de fin de curso**. Students begin saving money for the trip well in advance, and often have fund-raising activities to help cover costs. Imagine that you are an exchange student in one of the Spanish-speaking countries you have learned about this year. Use what you know about that country's history, culture, and geography to write a paragraph explaining where you think the class should go on its **excursión**. Say what you and your classmates could see and do in that place, and mention aspects like weather and cost to help convince the class.

_____

_____

_____

_____

_____

19 In the **Nota cultural** on p. 326 you read about the historic **paradores**. Spending the night at a **parador** can be fun, but it's not cheap. If you're traveling on a budget, there are cheaper possibilities. In Spain, your choices range from higher-priced **hoteles** to moderate **hostales** (*hostels* or *inns*), or from inexpensive **pensiones** to **casas de huéspedes** (*boarding houses*). All of these accommodations are rated with a set number of stars, according to what comforts they offer. So, you don't need to stay at a **parador** to be comfortable. Look over the advertisement for the Hotel "Cantabria". Then correct the statements that follow if they are false.

> ## Hotel "Cantabria" ★★
>
> Sólo un hotel ubicado en las montañas puede ofrecerle todas las comodidades para que descanse tranquilo. Aquí hay más de 30 habitaciones; todos con baño completo; televisión en color; teléfono.
>
> Salones para cursos y convenciones.
>
> Platos típicos.
>
> "Cantabria"; el nombre mismo invita al descanso, al disfrute de la naturaleza. El terreno verde presenta posibilidades de ocio por todo el año.
>
> - Excursiones de montaña.
> - Escalada.
> - Deportes acuáticos.
> - Parapente.
> - Deportes de invierno.
> - Ala delta.
>
> O, si lo prefiere, descanso absoluto.

1. The Hotel "Cantabria" is in the mountains.

_____

2. The hotel is very small, with only about 10 rooms.

_____

3. The hotel serves food.

_____

4. The rooms don't have televisions.

_____

5. The hotel is only open in the summer.

_____

EN MI CUADERNO

Describe an ideal friend, telling what he or she likes or dislikes. Include age, where the friend is from, and some activities he or she likes.

_____

_____

_____

_____

_____

_____

_____

_____

_____

_____

_____

_____

_____

_____

_____

_____

_____

_____

_____

_____

_____

_____

_____

_____

_____

■ EN MI CUADERNO

Next Monday is the first day of school. This weekend, you're going shopping. Write about what you already have and what you still need for school. You might want to include some other things you're thinking of buying for yourself.

_____

_____

_____

_____

_____

_____

_____

_____

_____

_____

_____

_____

_____

_____

_____

_____

_____

_____

_____

_____

_____

_____

_____

_____

■ EN MI CUADERNO

Write a letter describing yourself to a potential cabin mate at summer camp. Give your name and age. Describe both your physical traits and your personality. Include in your description an activity or two you like or don't like at school. Then ask for your potential cabin mate's age, personality, and likes and dislikes.

_____

_____

_____

_____

_____

_____

_____

_____

_____

_____

_____

_____

_____

_____

_____

_____

_____

_____

_____

_____

_____

_____

_____

_____

■ EN MI CUADERNO

You're making plans with a friend for next weekend. Create a conversation in which the two of you decide on the days, times, and activities you'll be doing, where you'll be going, and with whom.

_____
_____
_____
_____
_____
_____
_____
_____
_____
_____
_____
_____
_____
_____
_____
_____
_____
_____
_____
_____
_____
_____
_____
_____
_____
_____
_____

EN MI CUADERNO

Tell a pen pal what each season is like where you live and what activities you like to do with your friends during each of them. Then ask your pen pal what the climate is like where he or she lives.

_____

_____

_____

_____

_____

_____

_____

_____

_____

_____

_____

_____

_____

_____

_____

_____

_____

_____

_____

_____

_____

_____

_____

_____

■ EN MI CUADERNO

Describe your favorite relative. Write about his or her personality traits and what you enjoy doing together. Use an imaginary relative if you wish.

_____

_____

_____

_____

_____

_____

_____

_____

_____

_____

_____

_____

_____

_____

_____

_____

_____

_____

_____

_____

_____

_____

◼ EN MI CUADERNO

Tell the story of an ideal day from morning to evening. Tell what you plan to do, where you're going to go, when, and with whom.

_____

_____

_____

_____

_____

_____

_____

_____

_____

_____

_____

_____

_____

_____

_____

_____

_____

_____

_____

_____

_____

_____

_____

_____

_____

_____

_____

_____

EN MI CUADERNO

Write a conversation in which you order your ideal meal at your favorite restaurant. Tell the server why you like to go to this restaurant. As part of your conversation, ask the server how much the bill is and determine if you need to leave a tip on the table.

152 Practice and Activity Book

¡Ven conmigo! Level 1

HRW material copyrighted under notice appearing earlier in this work.

EN MI CUADERNO

Imagine that you've been in an accident and are going to be home for a week. Your friends and neighbors have offered to pick up your assignments and do your weekly chores and errands. Write a letter to one of your friends and explain what you need. Assign each of your friends a necessary task.

_____

_____

_____

_____

_____

_____

_____

_____

_____

_____

_____

_____

_____

_____

_____

_____

_____

_____

_____

_____

_____

_____

_____

_____

_____

_____

_____

CAPÍTULO 9 En mi cuaderno

EN MI CUADERNO

Describe your favorite holiday celebration of past years. Be as precise as you can, including time of year, who celebrated this special day with you, who decorated the house and sent the invitations, who came early or late, and if anyone danced, played music, or just talked a lot.

_____

_____

_____

_____

_____

_____

_____

_____

_____

_____

_____

_____

_____

_____

_____

_____

_____

_____

_____

_____

_____

_____

_____

_____

_____

EN MI CUADERNO

Describe what you and your friends like to do to stay healthy and take care of yourselves. Mention exercise, sleep, and eating habits in your description and tell how you feel when you do and don't stick to your program.

_____

_____

_____

_____

_____

_____

_____

_____

_____

_____

_____

_____

_____

_____

_____

_____

_____

_____

_____

_____

_____

_____

_____

CAPÍTULO 11 En mi cuaderno

EN MI CUADERNO

Describe an eventful trip you took. Give many details, telling where you went, with whom, and what happened. You may combine several trips in your description, or write about an imaginary one if you wish.

_____

_____

_____

_____

_____

_____

_____

_____

_____

_____

_____

_____

_____

_____

_____

_____

_____

_____

_____

_____

_____

_____

_____

_____

_____

_____

_____

_____